34

FISH

CARP, MINNOWS, AND ALLIES

Barbs, Goldfish, Suckers, Loaches ...

JOHN DAWES

GROLIER

an imprint of

SCHOLASTIC

www.scholastic.com/librarypublishing

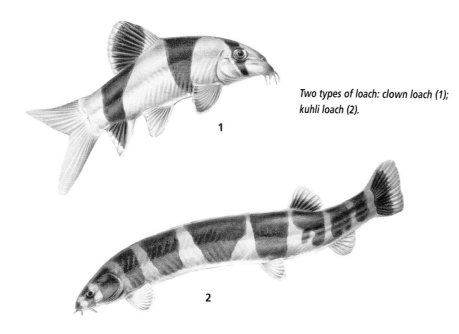

Two types of loach: clown loach (1); kuhli loach (2).

Published 2005 by Grolier, an imprint of
Scholastic Library Publishing
Danbury, CT 06816

This edition published exclusively for the school and library market

The Brown Reference Group plc.
(incorporating Andromeda Oxford Limited)
8 Chapel Place
Rivington Street
London EC2A 3DQ

Project Directors:	Graham Bateman, Lindsey Lowe
Editors:	Marion Dent, Andrew Stilwell, John Woodward
Art Editor and Designer:	Tony Truscott
Picture Managers:	Helen Simm, Becky Cox
Picture Researcher:	Alison Floyd
Main Artists:	Denys Ovenden, Mick Loates, Colin Newman
Indexers:	Michael and Marion Dent
Production:	Alastair Gourlay, Maggie Copeland

Printed in Singapore

Library of Congress Cataloging-in-Publication Data

Fish.
    p. cm. - - (World of Animals)
    Contents: vol. 31. Primitive fish -- vol. 32. Sharks -- vol. 33. Rays, chimaeras, and eels -- vol. 34. Carps, minnows, and allies -- vol. 35. Salmon, trout, and allies -- vol. 36. Cod, herring, and allies -- vol. 37. Catfish -- vol. 38. Piranhas -- vol. 39. Spiny-finned fish 1 -- vol. 40. Spiny-finned fish 2.
    ISBN 0-7172-5905-6 (set: alk. paper) -- ISBN 0-7172-5906-4 (vol. 31) -- ISBN 0-7172-5907-2 (vol. 32) --ISBN 0-7172-5908-0 (vol. 33) -- ISBN 0-7172-5909-9 (vol. 34) -- ISBN 0-7172-5910-2 (vol. 35) -- ISBN 0-7172-5911-0 (vol. 36) -- ISBN 0-7172-5912-9 (vol. 37) -- ISBN 0-7172-5913-7 (vol. 38) -- ISBN 0-7172-5914-5 (vol. 39) -- ISBN 0-7172-5915-3 (vol. 40)
    1. Fishes--Juvenile literature. I. Grolier (Firm) II. World of animals (Danbury, Conn.)

QL617.2.F55 2004
597--dc22

2004047333   Set ISBN 0-7172-5905-6

About This Volume

With the possible exception of the fish known as gobies, the 2,000-plus species of freshwater-bound carps and minnows make up the largest family (the Cyprinidae) of living vertebrates. They in turn form part of a large order of over 2,650 cypriniform, or carplike, fish—all of which are characterized by having scaleless heads and no teeth in their jaws. Some even lack a true stomach. The range of shapes, sizes, and habits found in cypriniform fish is so diverse that it is sometimes difficult to see how they can all belong to the same order. For example, cypriniform fish range from the familiar pet goldfish to the giant 9-foot (2.7-m) mahseers, and from the small, eel-like loaches—some of which "burp" in response to changing weather conditions—to the Chinese algae eater, which can hang onto a rock with its mouth in fast-flowing water while feeding and breathing at the same time. Then there are the unique bitterlings, which lay their eggs inside living freshwater mussels. Numerous other examples of diversity are found among the order. An ample selection of representatives from all the families in the order Cypriniformes is featured in this volume. They include both species that are widespread and abundant, as well as some, like the razorback sucker and some of the shiners and barbs, that are close to extinction.

2378

Contents

The grass carp gets its name because it eats vast quantities of aquatic plants.

Like many cyprinids, the Chinese algae eater (1), European barbel (2), and weather loach (3) have omnivorous diets.

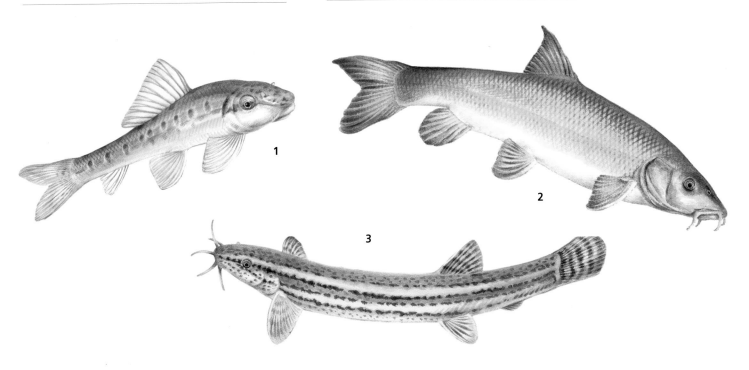

How to Use This Set

World of Animals: Fish is a 10-volume set that describes in detail fish from all around the world. Each volume features species that are grouped together because they share similar characteristics. So all the world's sharks are found in Volume 32, carplike fish are in Volume 34, catfish are in Volume 37, and so on. To help you find the volumes containing species that interest you, look at pages 6 and 7 (Find the Animal). A brief introduction to each volume is also given on page 2 (About This Volume).

Data panel presents basic statistics of fish or fish group

Red lyretail (*Aphyosemion bivittatum*)

.... *Image of animal or typical named example of group*

Common name Rivulines

Family Aplocheilidae

Subfamilies Aplocheilinae (Old World rivulines or killifish), Rivulinae (New World rivulines or killifish)

Order Cyprinodontiformes

Number of species Over 275 in 20 genera

Size From around 1.2 in (3 cm) to 2.8 in (7 cm)

Key features Elongated body; some South American *Cynolebias* deeper bodied; snout pointed, as in *Epiplatys* and *Aplocheilus*, or rounded in *Nothobranchius*; eyes large; mouth directed upward; fins well formed; no adipose fin; dorsal and anal fins set well back; tail rounded— extensions in some, e.g., clown killifish (*Epiplatys annulatus*); coloration variable in males— spectacular in many *Aphyosemion* and *Nothobranchius*; females drabber

Breeding Egg layers; spawning takes place continuously over several weeks; spawning in pairs; eggs laid on plants or buried in bottom mud; hatching from around 2 weeks to several months

Diet Small invertebrates, especially insects

Habitat Streams, ponds, and ditches; many in waters that dry up in summer season

Distribution Aplocheilinae: Africa, Indian subcontinent, Indo-Malayan archipelago; Rivulinae: southern Florida, Cuba into South America as far as Uruguay

Status Several under threat, primarily: Turner's gaucho (*Campellolebias brucei*) plus 7 *Cynolebias* species from Brazil—Vulnerable; Sakaramy panchax (*Pachypanchax sakaramyi*) from Madagascar— Vulnerable; Caprivi nothobranch (*Nothobranchius* species) from the Caprivi Strip in Namibia— Endangered

ⓘ *A native of equatorial Africa, the flamboyant male red lyretail (Aphyosemion bivittatum) is one of several species of killifish that have proved popular with aquarists.*

.... *Name and scientific classification of animal(s)*

.... *Sizes given in imperial units followed by metric equivalent*

.... *Basic description of animal(s), its life, and distribution*

.... *Conservation status if threatened (see Glossary)*

.... *Caption to image above if animal is part of a larger group*

Article Styles

Each volume contains two types of article. The first kind introduces major groups of fish (such as the ray-finned fish or the perchlike fish). This article reviews the variety of fish in the groups as well as their relationship with other groups of fish. The second type of article makes up most of each volume. It concentrates on describing in detail individual fish, such as the thornback ray, families of fish, such as hammerhead sharks, or groups of related families. Each such article starts with a fact-filled **data panel** to help you gather information at a glance. Used together, the two styles of article enable you to become familiar with specific fish in the context of their evolutionary history and biological relationships.

Article describes a particular fish or group of fish

Scientific name of animal

Common name of animal

Captions to photographs provide additional information about each animal's lifestyle

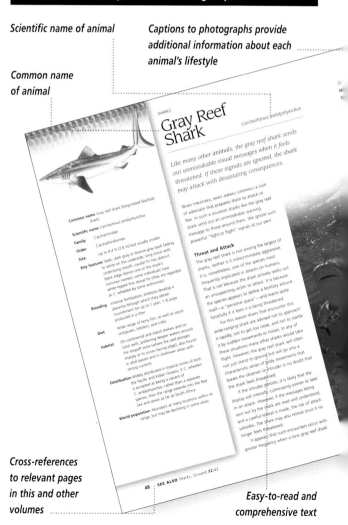

SHARKS
Gray Reef Shark
Carcharhinus bmblyrhynchos

Like many other animals, the gray reef shark sends out unmistakable visual messages when it feels threatened. If these signals are ignored, the shark may attack with devastating consequences.

Common name Gray reef shark (long-nosed blacktail shark)

Scientific name Carcharhinus amblyrhynchos

Family Carcharhinidae

Order Carcharhiniformes

Size Up to 8.4 ft (2.6 m) but usually smaller

Key features Sleek, dark-gray or bronze-gray back fading to white on the underside; long snout with underlying markings (hence one of the shark's common names); some individuals have white-tipped first dorsal fin (they are regarded as C. wheeleri by some authorities)

Breeding Internal fertilization; embryos develop a placenta through which they obtain nourishment for up to 1 year; 1–6 pups produced in a litter

Diet Wide range of bony fish, as well as squid, octopuses, lobsters, and crabs

Habitat On continental and island shelves and on coral reefs, preferring deeper waters around the dropoff zone (where the reef plunges sharply at its ocean-facing edge); also found in atoll passes and in shallower areas with strong currents

Distribution Widely distributed in tropical zones of both the Pacific and Indian Oceans; if C. wheeleri is accepted as being a variant of C. amblyrhynchos rather than a separate species, then the range extends into the Red Sea and down as far as South Africa

World population Abundant at many locations within its range, but may be declining in some areas

WHEN THREATENED, MANY ANIMALS EXPERIENCE a rush of adrenalin that prepares them to attack or flee. In such a situation sharks like the gray reef shark send out an unmistakable warning message to those around them. We ignore such powerful "fight or flight" signals at our peril.

Threat and Attack

The gray reef shark is not among the largest of sharks, neither is it indiscriminately aggressive. It is, nonetheless, one of the species most frequently implicated in attacks on humans. That is not because the shark actively seeks out an unsuspecting victim to attack. It is because the species appears to define a territory around itself—a "personal space"—and reacts quite forcefully if it feels it is being threatened.

For this reason divers that encounter this wide-ranging shark are advised not to approach it rapidly, not to get too close, and not to startle it by sudden movements or noises. In any of these situations many other sharks would take flight. However, the gray reef shark will often not just stand its ground but will go into a characteristic series of body movements that leaves the observer or intruder in no doubt that the shark feels threatened.

If the intruder persists, it is likely that the display will intensify, culminating sooner or later in an attack. However, if the messages being sent out by the shark are read and understood, and a careful retreat is made, the risk of attack subsides. The shark may also retreat once it no longer feels threatened.

It appears that such encounters occur with greater frequency when a lone gray reef shark

48 SEE ALSO Sharks, Ground 32:42

Cross-references to relevant pages in this and other volumes

Easy-to-read and comprehensive text

A number of other features help you navigate through the volumes and present you with helpful extra information. At the bottom of many pages are **cross-references** to other articles of interest. They may be to related fish, fish that live in similar places, fish with similar behavior, predators (or prey), and much more. Each volume also contains a **Set Index** to the complete *World of Animals: Fish*. Most fish mentioned in the text are indexed by common and scientific names, and many topics are also covered. There is also a **Glossary** that will help you if there are words in the text that you do not fully understand. Each volume includes a list of useful **Further Reading and Websites** that help you take your research further. On page 7 you will find a complete checklist of all the fish superclasses, classes, and orders of the world and where they are featured in the set.

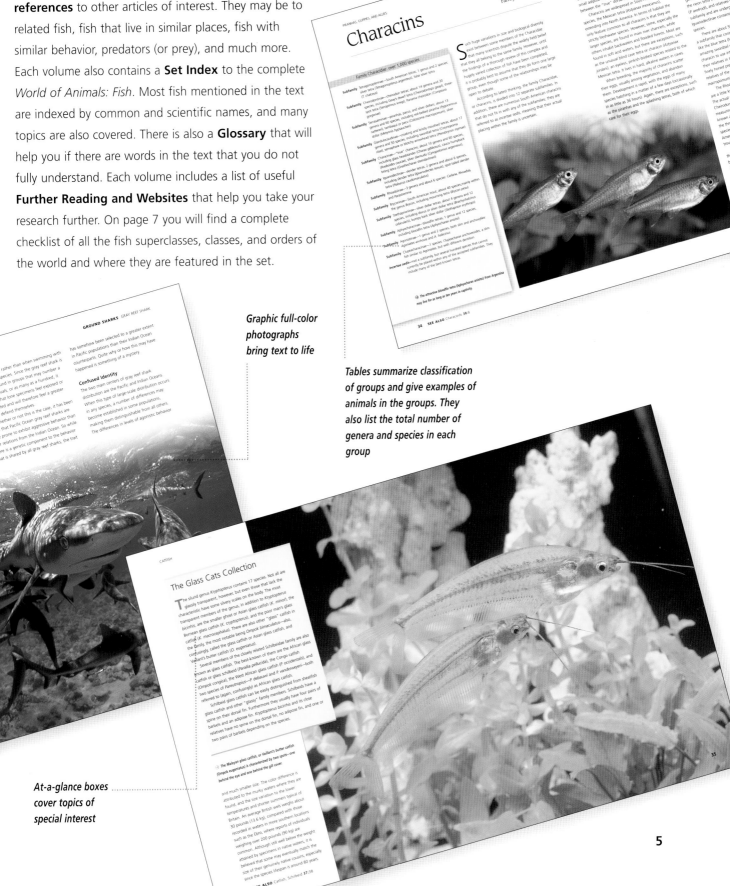

Graphic full-color photographs bring text to life

Tables summarize classification of groups and give examples of animals in the groups. They also list the total number of genera and species in each group

At-a-glance boxes cover topics of special interest

Introductory article describes groups of closely related fish

Family Characidae

PIRANHAS, GUPPIES, AND ALLIES

Characins

Such huge variations in size and biological diversity exist between some members of the Characidae that many scientists dispute the widely held belief that they all belong to the same family. However, until the findings of a thorough review of this complex and hugely varied collection of fish have been completed, it is probably best to assume that they do form one large group, even though some of the relationships may be open to debate.

Characins are widespread in South America, with one species, the Mexican tetra (*Astyanax mexicanus*), extending into North America. In terms of habitat the only feature common to all characins is that they are strictly freshwater species. However, some, especially the larger species, are found in main river channels, while others inhabit backwaters and flooded forests. Most are found in soft acid waters, but there are exceptions, such as the unusual blind cave tetra or characin (*Astyanax jordani*), an eyeless, pinkish-bodied species related to the Mexican tetra. It lives in hard, alkaline waters in caves.

When breeding, the majority of characins scatter their eggs, usually among vegetation, and abandon them. Development is rapid, with the eggs of many species hatching in a matter of a few days (occasionally in as little as 36 hours). Again, there are exceptions, such as the pirahnas and the splashing tetras, both of which care for their eggs.

Characin Characteristics

Most characins have the characteristics described for the order Characiformes. Among the most obvious is the presence of sharp, well-formed teeth, even in the smallest species. The vast majority of species also have a small adipose fin—the small, second dorsal located between the "true" dorsal and the tail.

According to latest thinking, the family Characidae, or characins, is divided into 12 separate subfamilies. In addition, there are numerous South American characins that do not fit in with any of the subfamilies; they are referred to as *incertae sedis*, meaning that their actual placing within the family is uncertain.

The Subfamilies

The Characinae, or "true" characins, contains genera and 60 species. The best known headstander (*Charax gibbosus*) and their relatives (*Roeboides* species) and their relatives, chunky species with an obvious hump...

The South American tetras in the Tetragonopterinae used to be a... However, it now includes just a... genus Tetragonopterus. Most of... the neon tetra (*Paracheirodon* species and relatives—well as the glassy bloodfin (*Prionobrama*)...

Family Characidae: over 1,000 species	
Subfamily	Tetragonopterinae—South American tetras. 1 genus and 2 species; silver tetra (*Tetragonopterus argenteus*), false silver tetra (*T. chalceus*)
Subfamily	Cheirodontinae—cheirodon tetras; about 14 genera and 30 species, including Gray's dwarf tetra (*Cheirodontops geayi*), three-spot tetra (*Serrapinnus kriegi*), Panama cheirodon (*Compsura gorgonae*)
Subfamily	Serrasalminae—piranhas, pacus, and silver dollars; about 13 genera and 60 species, including red-bellied piranha (*Pygocentrus nattereri*), tambaqui or pacu (*Colossoma macropomum*), silver dollar (*Metynnis hypsauchen*)
Subfamily	Glandulocaudinae—croaking and bristly mouthed tetras; about 17 genera and 50 species, including swordtail tetra (*Corynopoma riisei*), semaphore or blotchy arrowhead tetra (*Pterobrycon myrnae*)
Subfamily	Characinae—"true" characins; about 10 genera and 60 species, including glass headstander (*Charax gibbosus*), cauca humpback (*Roeboides caucae*), dawn characin (*Gymnocorymbus argenteus*), biting tetra (*Gnathocharax steindachneri*)
Subfamily	Iguanodectinae—slender tetras; 2 genera and about 6 species, including slender tetra (*Piabucus caudomaculatus*)
Subfamily	Rhoadsiinae—3 genera and about 6 species; Carlana, Rhoadsia, and Parastremma
Subfamily	Bryconinae—South American trout; including mounting tetra (*Brycon pesu*) and the genus *Brycon*, including mounting tetra about 40 species, mainly within...
Subfamily	Stethaprioninae—silver dollar tetras; about 4 genera and 12 species, including discus or silver dollar tetra (*Brachychalcinus orbicularis*), bumpy back silver dollar (*Stethaprion erythrops*)
Subfamily	Aphyocharacinae—bloodfin tetras; 1 genus and 12 species, including bloodfin tetra (*Aphyocharax anisitsi*)
Subfamily	Agoneatinae—1 genus and 2 species; both slim and anchovylike
Subfamily	Clupeacharacinae—1 species. Clupeacharax anchoveoides, a slim fish similar to Agoneates, both with different dentition
Incertae sedis	—not a subfamily, but several hundred species that cannot currently be placed within any of the accepted subfamilies. They include many of the best-known tetras.

⊙ *The attractive bloodfin tetra (Aphyocharax anisitsi) from Argentina may live for as long as ten years in captivity.*

34 SEE ALSO Characids 38:6

GROUND SHARKS GRAY REEF SHARK

...3 rather than when swimming with ...species. Since the gray reef shark is ...und in groups that may number a ...duals, or as many as a hundred, it ...that lone specimens feel exposed or ...cted and will therefore feel a greater ...defend themselves.

...whether or not this is the case, it has been ...that Pacific Ocean gray reef sharks are ...e prone to exhibit aggressive behavior than ...r relations from the Indian Ocean. So while ...ere is a genetic component to the behavior ...at is shared by all gray reef sharks, the trait

...has somehow been selected to a greater extent in Pacific populations than their Indian Ocean counterparts. Quite why or how this may have happened is something of a mystery.

Confused Identity

The two main centers of gray reef shark distribution are the Pacific and Indian Oceans. When this type of large-scale distribution occurs in any species, a number of differences may become established in some populations, making them distinguishable from all others. The differences in levels of agonistic behavior

---

CATFISH

The Glass Cats Collection

The silurid genus *Kryptopterus* contains 17 species. Not all are glassily transparent, however, but even those that lack the characteristic have some silvery scales on the body. The most transparent members of the genus, in addition to *Kryptopterus bicirrhis*, are the smaller ghost or Asian glass catfish (*K. minor*), the Bornean glass catfish (*K. cryptopterus*), and the poor man's glass catfish (*K. macrocephalus*). There are also other "glass" catfish in the family, the most notable being Ompok bimaculatus—also, confusingly, called the glass catfish or Asian glass catfish, and Vaillant's butter catfish (*O. eugeniatus*).

Several members of the closely related Schilbeidae family are also known as glass catfish. The best-known of them are the African glass catfish or glass schilbeid (*Parailia pellucida*), the Congo catfish (*Ompok congica*), the West African glass catfish (*P. occidentalis*), and two species of *Pareutropius—P. debauwi* and *P. vanderweyeni*—both referred to (again, confusingly) as African glass catfish.

Schilbeid glass catfish can be easily distinguished from sheatfish glass catfish and other "glassy" family members. Schilbeids have a spine on their dorsal fin. Furthermore they usually have four pairs of barbels and an adipose fin. Kryptopterus bicirrhis and its close relatives have no spine on the dorsal fin, no adipose fin, and one or two pairs of barbels depending on the species.

⊙ *The Malayan glass catfish, or Vaillant's butter catfish (Ompok eugeniatus) is characterized by two spots—one behind the eye and one behind the gill cover.*

...and much smaller size. The color difference is attributed to the murky waters where they are found, and the size variation to the lower temperatures and shorter summers typical of Britain. An average British wels weighs about 30 pounds (13.6 kg), compared with those recorded in waters in more southern locations such as the Ebro, where reports of individuals weighing over 200 pounds (90 kg) are common. Although still well below the weight attained by specimens in native waters, it is believed that some may eventually match the size of their genuinely native cousins, especially since the species lifespan is around 80 years.

SEE ALSO Catfish, Schilbed 37:18

Find the Animal

World of Animals: *Fish* is the fourth part of a library that describes all groups of living animals. Each cluster of volumes in *World of Animals* covers a familiar group of animals—mammals, birds, reptiles, amphibians, fish, and insects and other invertebrates. These groups also represent categories of animals recognized by scientists (see The Animal Kingdom below).

Rank	Scientific name	Common name
Phylum	Chordata	Animals with a backbone
Superclass	Gnathostomata	Jawed fish
Class	Actinopterygii	Ray-finned fish
Order	Characiformes	Characoids
Family	Characidae	Characins
Genus	*Pygocentrus*	Piranhas
Species	*natereri*	Red-bellied piranha

The Animal Kingdom

The living world is divided into five kingdoms, one of which (kingdom Animalia) is the main subject of the *World of Animals*. Kingdom Animalia is divided into numerous major groups called phyla, but only one of them (Chordata) contains animals that have a backbone. Chordates, or vertebrates, include animals like mammals, birds, reptiles, amphibians, and fish. There are about 38,000 species of vertebrates, while the phyla that contain animals without backbones (so-called invertebrates, like insects and spiders) include at least 1 million species. To find which set of volumes in the *World of Animals* you need to choose, see the chart below.

The kingdom Animalia is subdivided into groups such as classes, families, genera, and species. Above is the classification of the red-bellied piranha.

Fish in Particular

World of Animals: Fish provides a broad survey of some of the most abundant, unusual, varied, and yet rarely seen creatures on our planet. Fish are unique among vertebrates because all species live in water—although some have adapted to spend periods on land. Fish are

divided into major groups called superclasses, classes, and orders. The two superclasses comprise the jawless and the jawed fish. Different classes include fish such as lobe-finned fish, cartilaginous fish, and ray-finned fish. In each class there are often a number of fish orders, and in the orders there are families. All the fish superclasses, classes, and orders are shown on page 7; the common names of some of the most important species in these groups are also listed.

Fish classification is a changing science. Not only have several different ways of grouping fish already been proposed, but new evidence, such as from DNA analysis, has resulted in a major rethinking of the fish family tree;

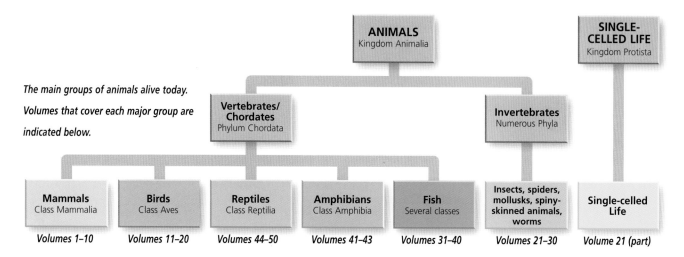

The main groups of animals alive today. Volumes that cover each major group are indicated below.

| ANIMALS Kingdom Animalia | | | | | | SINGLE-CELLED LIFE Kingdom Protista |

Vertebrates/Chordates — Phylum Chordata | Invertebrates — Numerous Phyla

| Mammals Class Mammalia | Birds Class Aves | Reptiles Class Reptilia | Amphibians Class Amphibia | Fish Several classes | Insects, spiders, mollusks, spiny-skinned animals, worms | Single-celled Life |
| Volumes 1–10 | Volumes 11–20 | Volumes 44–50 | Volumes 41–43 | Volumes 31–40 | Volumes 21–30 | Volume 21 (part) |

the result is that some species are now placed in different groups by different scientists. Furthermore, the same fish may have a different name under different systems of classification. Therefore the system of classification in this set may differ from others and may itself change as the results of new studies emerge. The system followed mostly here is the one devised by Joseph S. Nelson in *Fishes of the World* (John Wiley & Sons, Inc., 1994).

Naming Fish

To discuss animals, names are needed for the different kinds. Red-bellied piranhas are one kind of fish and black-spot piranhas another. All red-bellied piranhas look alike, breed together, and produce young like themselves. This distinction corresponds closely to the zoologists' definition of a species. All red-bellied piranhas belong to one species, and all black-spot piranhas belong to another species.

Most animals have different names in different languages. Therefore zoologists use an internationally recognized system for naming species consisting of two-word scientific names, usually in Latin or Greek. The red-bellied piranha is called *Pygocentrus natereri* and the black-spot piranha *Pygocentrus cariba*. *Pygocentrus* is the name of the genus (a group of very similar species) that includes red-bellied and black-spot piranhas; *natereri* or *cariba* indicates the species in the genus. The same scientific names are recognized the world over. This allows for precision and helps avoid confusion. However, a species may have more than one scientific name—it may have been described and named at different times without the zoologists realizing it was one species.

FISH SUPERCLASSES, CLASSES, AND ORDERS

SUPERCLASS AGNATHA	**jawless fish**
Order Petromyzontiformes **(Vol. 31)**	lampreys
Order Myxiniformes **(Vol. 31)**	hagfish
SUPERCLASS GNATHOSTOMATA	**jawed fish**
CLASS CHONDRICHTHYES	**cartilaginous fish**
Order Heterodontiformes **(Vol. 32)**	bullhead sharks
Order Orectolobiformes **(Vol. 32)**	carpet sharks
Order Carcharhiniformes **(Vol. 32)**	ground sharks
Order Lamniformes **(Vol. 32)**	mackerel sharks
Order Hexanchiformes **(Vol. 32)**	frilled and cow sharks
Order Squaliformes **(Vol. 32)**	dogfish sharks
Order Squatiniformes **(Vol. 32)**	angel sharks
Order Pristiophoriformes **(Vol. 32)**	saw sharks
Order Rajiformes **(Vol. 33)**	rays
Order Chimaeriformes **(Vol. 33)**	chimaeras
CLASS SARCOPTERYGII	**lobe-finned fish**
Order Coelacanthiformes **(Vol. 31)**	coelacanths
Order Ceratodontiformes **(Vol. 31)**	Australian lungfish
Order Lepidosireniformes **(Vol. 31)**	South American and African lungfish
CLASS ACTINOPTERYGII	**ray-finned fish**
Order Polypteriformes **(Vol. 31)**	bichirs and ropefish
Order Acipenseriformes **(Vol. 31)**	sturgeons and paddlefish
Order Amiiformes **(Vol. 31)**	bowfin
Order Semionotiformes **(Vol. 31)**	garfish
Order Osteoglossiformes **(Vol. 31)**	bonytongues and allies
Order Elopiformes **(Vol. 31)**	tarpons
Order Albuliformes **(Vol. 33)**	spiny eels
Order Anguilliformes **(Vol. 33)**	eels
Order Saccopharyngiformes **(Vol. 33)**	swallow and gulper eels

Order Clupeiformes **(Vol. 36)**	herring and allies
Order Cypriniformes **(Vol. 34)**	carp and minnows
Order Characiformes **(Vol. 38)**	characins and allies
Order Siluriformes **(Vol. 37)**	catfish
Order Gymnotiformes **(Vol. 33)**	New World knifefish
Order Esociformes **(Vol. 35)**	pikes, pickerels, and mudminnows
Order Osmeriformes **(Vol. 35)**	smelts and allies
Order Salmoniformes **(Vol. 35)**	salmon, trout, and allies
Order Stomiiformes **(Vol. 35)**	dragonfish and allies
Order Ateleopodiformes **(Vol. 35)**	jellynose fish
Order Aulopiformes **(Vol. 35)**	lizardfish
Order Myctophiformes **(Vol. 35)**	lanternfish
Order Lampridiformes **(Vol. 35)**	oarfish
Order Polymixiiformes **(Vol. 35)**	beardfish
Order Percopsiformes **(Vol. 36)**	trout-perches and allies
Order Ophidiiformes **(Vol. 36)**	cusk eels and brotulas
Order Gadiformes **(Vol. 36)**	cod and allies
Order Batrachoidiformes **(Vol. 36)**	toadfish
Order Lophiiformes **(Vol. 36)**	anglerfish and allies
Order Mugiliformes **(Vol. 38)**	mullets
Order Atheriniformes **(Vol. 38)**	rainbowfish and silversides
Order Beloniformes **(Vol. 38)**	flying fish and ricefish
Order Cyprinodontiformes **(Vol. 38)**	piranhas, guppies, and allies
Order Stephanoberyciformes **(Vol. 39)**	pricklefish and allies
Order Beryciformes **(Vol. 39)**	fangtooths and allies
Order Zeiformes **(Vol. 39)**	dories and allies
Order Gasterosteiformes **(Vol. 39)**	sticklebacks, sea horses, and allies
Order Synbranchiformes **(Vol. 33)**	swamp eels and allies
Order Mastacembeliformes **(Vol. 33)**	spiny eels
Order Scorpaeniformes **(Vol. 39)**	mail-cheeked fish
Order Perciformes **(Vol. 40)**	perchlike fish
Order Pleuronectiformes **(Vol. 39)**	flatfish
Order Tetraodontiformes **(Vol. 39)**	triggers, puffers, and allies

CYPRINIFORMS

The cypriniforms, comprising the order Cypriniformes, are a large group consisting of over 2,662 species. They include some of the best known of all fish, including the common carp (*Cyprinus carpio carpio*) and its ornamental varieties, the koi, plus the ever-popular goldfish (*Carassius auratus auratus*), widely regarded as the most popular pet in the world.

Just three features separate this large collection of species from all others. First, the heads of all but a very few species of cypriniforms lack scales. Second, cypriniforms are regarded as "toothless" because they do not have teeth of any kind on the upper or lower jaws. However, they do have pharyngeal teeth in the throat, which are mainly used to grind food particles. Third, with the exception of a few loaches, cypriniforms lack an adipose fin—the small "second dorsal" fin typical of many catfish and virtually all the characoids (see Volumes 37 and 38, respectively, of this set of books).

The order Cypriniformes includes many species that look so different from each other that they appear at first sight to be totally unrelated. There is, for example, the golden mahseer (*Tor putitora*)—a giant, barblike fish from

India that can grow to around 9 feet (2.7 m) in length and occurs in large, fast-flowing rivers. Then there are the eel-like kuhli loaches (*Pangio* species) that only grow to a few inches in length and spend most of the daylight hours hiding in the smallest crevices or buried in fine-grained sediments. In between these extremes is an array of species with wide-ranging body shapes and fascinating lifestyles and biology.

⊕ *The common carp (Cyprinus carpio carpio) is found almost globally from western Europe to Southeast Asia, both in large, slow-flowing rivers and still waters. It can grow to a size of 47 inches (1.2 m). It is often termed the "cunning carp" for its wariness when fully grown.*

Who's Who among the Cypriniforms?

Superfamily Cyprinoidea
  Family Cyprinidae—carps, minnows, and allies
    Subfamily Cyprininae—carps, minnows, barbs, "sharks", and relatives
    Subfamily Gobioninae—gudgeons and relatives
    Subfamily Rasborinae or Danioninae—rasboras, danios, white cloud mountain minnow, and relatives
    Subfamily Acheilognathinae—bitterlings
    Subfamily Leuciscinae—ide/orfe, rudds, roaches, breams, shiners, daces, tench
    Subfamily Cultrinae—*Culter, Parabramis,* and relatives
    Subfamily Alburninae—bleak and relatives
    Subfamily Psilorhynchinae—2 genera: *Psilorhynchoides* and *Psilorhynchus*
Superfamily Cobitoidea
  Family Gyrinocheilidae—algae eaters (4 species)
  Family Catostomidae—suckers
    Subfamily Ictiobinae—2 genera: *Carpiodes* (quillback and carpsuckers); *Ictiobus* (buffalo suckers)
    Subfamily Cycleptinae—Chinese sailfin sucker (*Myxocyprinus asiaticus*); blue sucker (*Cycleptus elongatus*)
    Subfamily Catostominae
      Tribe Catostomini—longnose sucker (*Catostomus catostomus*), razorback sucker (*Xyrauchen texanus*) and relatives
      Tribe Moxostomatini—chubsuckers, redhorse suckers, and relatives
  Family Cobitidae—loaches
    Subfamily Cobitinae—kuhli loaches, weather loaches, horse-faced loach, spined loach, and relatives
    Subfamily Botiinae—botia loaches, including clown loach and relatives
  Family Balitoridae or Homalopteridae—river loaches
    Subfamily Noemacheilinae or Nemacheilinae—stone loach and relatives
      Tribe Gastromyzontini—Hong Kong pleco and relatives
    Subfamily Balitorinae—flat loaches
      Tribe Balitorini—saddled hillstream loach and relatives

Amazing Bones

Cypriniforms have a specialized structure called a Weberian apparatus. The same structure is also found in catfish (order Siluriformes), characoids (order Characiformes), milkfish (family Chanidae), mudhead (family Phractolaemidae), and the South American knifefish and their relatives (order Gymnotiformes). The Weberian apparatus is considered to be such a significant shared characteristic that all the fish that have it together form the superorder Ostariophysi.

The Weberian apparatus consists of a series of small bones that link the skull with the swim bladder. More specifically, the bones concerned are four or five individual vertebrae (back bones) that have become highly modified through evolution to the extent that they no longer function exclusively as vertebrae.

Instead, parts of these bones have separated from the main part of the bone and now form a linked "chain" of tiny bones, or ossicles, on each side of the central axis of the backbone. The individual ossicles are known (from front to back) as the claustrum, scaphium, intercalarium, and tripus. The claustrum is linked to the inner ear of the fish, located in the skull, and the tripus is linked to the front end of the swim bladder, located in the space under the first few ribs.

When sound waves strike the body of a fish that has a Weberian apparatus, the sound waves make the swim bladder vibrate. The vibrations are passed on to the tripus, intercalarium, scaphium, and then—via the claustrum— to the inner ear of the fish. Owing to the shape of the individual ossicles, the vibrations are amplified as they move from the swim bladder to the inner ear. As a result, fish with a Weberian apparatus have a good sense of hearing. The ability to detect sound varies from order to order, family to family, or species to species. However, even the milkfish, mudhead, and their relatives within the order Gonorhynchiformes, which have a primitive Weberian arrangement involving only the first three vertebrae, have reasonable hearing ability when compared to most fish that do not have a Weberian apparatus.

The Families

There are five families of cypriniform fish, split between two superfamilies. The superfamily Cyprinoidea has a single family, the Cyprinidae, consisting of the carps, minnows, and their numerous allies. The second

superfamily, the Cobitoidea, contains the remaining four families: the algae eaters (family Gyrinocheilidae), the suckers (family Catostomidae), the loaches (family Cobitidae), and the river loaches (family Balitoridae, sometimes referred to as the family Homalopteridae).

⊕ *Koi, a variety of the common carp (Cyprinus carpio carpio), demonstrate the bewitching array of colors that make them such a favorite in ornamental fish collections. As well as being available in different colors, koi have been developed with a wide range of scale modifications, too.*

Cyprinids

The Cyprinidae is the largest family of freshwater fish. After the gobies (family Gobiidae) it is probably the second largest family of vertebrates (backboned animals). In fact, it is considered to be artificially large by some scientists who think that some of the fish generally considered as cyprinids may not in fact be so.

According to the system of fish classification set out by Nelson (1994), there are over 2,000 species in the family Cyprinidae. Not surprisingly, opinions differ on how they should be grouped. According to the version followed here, the family is divided into eight subfamilies. They are unequal in size (the Cyprininae, for instance, contains some 700 species, including over 100 species of barb, while the Psilorhynchinae contains just five), but all share a sufficient number of characteristics to be deemed members of a single family.

In addition, of course, they each have their own combination of characteristics that sets them apart within their own subfamilies. For example, in the bitterlings (subfamily Acheilognathinae) females develop long egg-laying tubes (known as ovipositors) with which they lay their eggs inside the body cavities of freshwater mussels. No other cyprinids have evolved this unusual breeding strategy, as a result of which the 14 or 15 species of known bitterlings are placed in a subfamily by themselves.

Algae Eaters

The algae eaters (Gyrinocheilidae) constitute one of the four families that together form the superfamily Cobitoidea. There are only four species in the Gyrinocheilidae, one of which, the Chinese algae eater or sucking loach (*Gyrinocheilus aymonieri*), is a very popular aquarium fish. In the wild the Chinese algae eater is truly remarkable for the way in which it can simultaneously cling to rocks in fast-flowing currents, feed, and breathe in oxygen.

Suckers

Somewhat larger in terms of numbers of species, as well as in general body size (at least in the majority of cases), is the family Catostomidae, with nearly 70 species. The suckers are mainly distributed across the North American landmass, with two notable exceptions: the longnose sucker (*Catostomus catostomus*), which occurs not just in North America but also in Siberia, and the majestic

Chinese sailfin sucker (*Myxocyprinus asiaticus*), which only occurs in China.

Suckers are interesting fish: Despite the large size some species can reach (around 40 inches/1 m), they feed on small invertebrates that they "vacuum" up from fine sediments—hence their name. Almost 30 species of suckers are under varying degrees of threat in the wild.

The Catostomidae is divided into four subfamilies, based largely on skeletal differences. For example, the Chinese sailfin sucker and its closest relative, the blue

sucker (*Cycleptus elongatus*), have higher numbers of dorsal fin rays than other suckers: The Chinese sailfin sucker has between 52 and 57 rays. In one of the subfamilies (the Catostominae) the species are divided into two tribes, largely depending on the number of scales along the lateral line organ (the sensory apparatus along the sides of a fish's body that detects waterborne vibrations). Species in the tribe Catostomini have more than 50 lateral line scales, while their relatives in the Moxostomatini have fewer than 50.

Loaches

Loaches (family Cobitidae) have elongated bodies that vary from spindle-shaped (tapering at both ends) to eel-like or wormlike. Loaches also have a spine under the eye (or in front of the eye in *Acanthopsis* species) that they can raise and three to six pairs of barbels.

⊕ *The lemonfin barb (Hypsibarbus vernayi), a member of the family Cyprinidae, shows its distinctive "lemon-slice" fins that distinguish it from the tinfoil barb (Barbonymus schwanenfeldii).*

There are some 110 or so species of loaches in total, which are subdivided into two subfamilies, according to Nelson (1994). The Cobitinae are all eel-like or wormlike in shape to varying degrees. Perhaps the best-known species are the weather loaches (*Misgurnus* species). They are named for their ability to "forecast" the weather by sensing, and reacting to, the drop in barometric pressure that precedes a storm. At such times these loaches become hyperactive and may even break wind!

The wormlike kuhli loaches also belong to this subfamily, along with members of about another 13 genera; in total there are about 70 species in the subfamily. The 40 or so members of the second subfamily, the Botinae, are not as elongated as the Cobitinae; the body is also considerably more flattened from side to side. Among the species are some beautiful representatives like the clown loach (*Botia macracanthus*) and the strikingly colored redtail loach (*B. modesta*), which has a bluish body to contrast with its tail.

River Loaches

Members of the family Balitoridae, the river loaches, are generally found in flowing water; some species live in torrential hillstreams. There are about 470 species, although not all experts agree about the number. In fact, some authorities place large numbers of species, for example, the stone loach (*Noemacheilus barbatulus*) and its relatives, in the kuhli loach family, the Cobitidae.

According to the Nelson's 1994 classification, the family Balitoridae is subdivided into two subfamilies. The stone loach and its relatives are placed in the subfamily Noemacheilinae, or Nemacheilinae. Their distinguishing characteristics include the lack of an eye spine and having three pairs of barbels. Their body shape is generally elongated but not flattened top to bottom.

Members of the second subfamily (the Balitorinae) are usually referred to as the flat loaches owing to their overall body shape. However differences between them mean that the subfamily is further divided into two tribes. The tribe Balitorini contains species like the attractively marked saddled hillstream loach (*Homaloptera orthogoniata*) and its closest relatives. Together, the 13 genera in the tribe consist of moderately elongated fish. Although they are flattish in general body shape, especially at the front, they are nowhere as flat as their counterparts in the tribe Gastromyzontini. These fish, many of which live in high-energy habitats like torrents, have flat front ends, suckerlike mouths, and pectoral and pelvic fins modified into suction devices that allow them to cling in conditions where most other fish would be swept away.

⊕ *The slimy, or Myer's loach (*Pangio myersi*), a member of the family Cobitidae, is not normally seen during daylight hours, when it either buries itself under the sandy substrate or hides between rocks. It is expert at seeking out small particles of food in the dark.*

Carps and Minnows

Family Cyprinidae

The carps, minnows, and their relatives form the family Cyprinidae within the order Cypriniformes. It is the largest of the exclusively freshwater families of fish. Along with the gobies (family Gobiidae), which are found in fresh water, brackish, and marine environments, the cyprinids also form one of the largest families of vertebrates (backboned animals) alive today. Among the 2,010 or so species are some of the best known of all freshwater fish, including the goldfish (*Carassius auratus auratus*), common carp (*Cyprinus carpio carpio*), and minnows (*Phoxinus* species). With such a large number of species and such a wide distribution in Eurasia, North America, and Africa, it is not surprising that the carp and minnow family exhibits a great diversity of shape, size, and characteristics.

It is also hardly surprising, therefore, that there is a great deal of debate regarding the actual composition of the family. In fact, many scientists believe that the family is "artificially" large. Most agree that it should be divided into a number of subfamilies, but opinions vary as to how this should be done.

It is even difficult to select characteristics that are shared by all members of the family, and that distinguish them from all other families. For example, cyprinids have an extendible mouth with toothless jaws, although they have teeth on their pharyngeal ("throat") bones. They also exhibit a number of skull bone and muscle modifications, along with two pairs of mouth barbels (but not in all species) and a scaleless head (cyprinids are often said to be bald), but they lack an adipose ("second dorsal") fin.

The difficulty with using one, or a combination, of these features to identify a fish as belonging to the family Cyprinidae is that none of the characteristics is unique to carps and their relatives. Furthermore, all of them, plus others, are shared with the other families that together constitute the order Cypriniformes.

Fish Eaters to Algae Crunchers

Despite the wide range of shapes and sizes found among cyprinids, only two genera contain species that feed exclusively on other fish: the North American squawfish (*Ptychocheilus* species) and the giant yellow cheek (*Elopichthys bambusa*) from China and the Amur River, which grows to around 6.6 feet (2 m). This does not mean that they are the only two predatory genera in the family: Many other genera and species also include fish in their diet, but they also supplement them to a larger or lesser extent with terrestrial and aquatic insects and other invertebrates. The larger species may also eat amphibians and other vertebrates as well.

At the other end of the feeding spectrum some

Family Cyprinidae: 210–220 genera, 2,010 species, 8 subfamilies

Subfamily Cyprininae—from Eurasia and Africa; genera include *Barbus* (barbels, barbs), *Carassius* (goldfish, crucian carp), *Ctenopharyngodon* (grass carp), *Cyprinus* (common carp, koi), *Labeo* and *Epalzeorhynchos* (freshwater "sharks"), *Tor* (mahseers)

Subfamily Gobioninae—from eastern Asia and Eurasia; genera include *Gobio* (gudgeons)

Subfamily Rasborinae—from Africa and southern Eurasia; genera include *Danio* (danios), *Rasbora* (rasboras), *Tanichthys* (White Cloud Mountain minnow)

Subfamily Acheilognathinae—from Eurasia; genera include *Rhodeus* (bitterlings)

Subfamily Leuciscinae—from North America and Eurasia; genera include *Cyprinella* (shiners), *Leuciscus* (ide, European chub, common dace), *Phoxinus* (Eurasian minnow, American dace), *Rutilus* (roach), *Scardinius* (rudd), *Tinca* (tench)

Subfamily Cultrinae—from Eastern Asia; genera include *Culter*, *Parabramis*

Subfamily Alburninae—from Europe and Asia; genera include *Alburnus* (bleak)

Subfamily Psilorhynchinae—from Nepal, India, to western Myanmar; genera include *Psilorhynchus* (torrent loaches)

⊖ *The red-tailed black shark (Epalzeorhynchos bicolor) is so called due to its dramatic appearance. It can grow to about 12 inches (30 cm).*

species feed almost exclusively on free-floating algae that they filter from the water. One of the best examples of such a filter feeder is the silver carp (*Hypophthalmichthys molitrix*) from China and the Amur basin. "Sharks," such as the red-tailed black shark (*Epalzeorhynchos bicolor*), and flying foxes like the Siamese flying fox (*Crossocheilus siamensis*) also feed on algae, but not on the free-floating types; they scrape encrusting algae from rocks and plants instead. Other vegetarian cyprinids feed on larger plants, perhaps the best known being the aptly named grass carp (*Ctenopharyngodon idellus*), which also comes from China and the Amur basin.

In between the strict herbivores (plant eaters), on the one hand, and the piscivores (fish eaters) and carnivores (flesh eaters), on the other, lie the omnivores—species

that eat a wide range of foods, including both plant and animal matter. The widespread and well-known common carp (*Cyprinus carpio carpio*) is one of many such omnivorous species.

From Dwarves to Giants

There are so many species in the Cyprinidae, with such varied eating habits, widely ranging distributions, and diversity of habitats, that this is bound to be reflected in their size range. In fact, some of the smallest and some of the largest of all freshwater fish species belong to this extensive family.

At the bottom end of the size spectrum, for example, there is a tiny daniolike fish from Burma known as *Danionella translucida*, the females of which mature at

⊖ *Leaping barbs* (Chela caeruleostigmata) *have an unusual technique for escaping from their enemies: They flick their heads backward, exerting a force in the water that propels them rapidly forward.*

around 6.6 feet (2 m) and a weight of nearly 90 pounds (40 kg), and the putitor, golden mahseer, or large-scaled barb (*Tor putitora*) from the Brahmaputra River in eastern India, capable of growing to just over 9 feet (2.7 m). Among the American cyprinids the largest is the Colorado squawfish (*Ptychocheilus lucius*), which grows to 6 feet (1.8 m) and can weigh in at 100 pounds (45 kg).

Some cyprinids are capable of living for considerable lengths of time. Precise data is not available for many species, however, and even when it is, it can sometimes be misleading. For example, a particular koi—an ornamental variety of the common carp—was long believed to have reached the venerable age of 223 years. However, later studies revealed that its age was closer to 50 years, although even this is still a considerable age by fish standards.

The Head Benders

Head raising or bending is very rare in fish, despite its widespread occurrence in other animals, from amphibians to mammals. However, two of these rare examples occur in the cyprinids. In the winged rasboras, Asian hatchetfish, or oriental white minnows (*Chela* species) from Southeast Asia the head can be flexed backward with such speed and force that it projects the fish in the opposite direction, in other words, forward. It is believed that head propulsion can be used as a rapid escape mechanism when the fish are threatened in some way.

In *Macrochirichthys* species the large mouth points at a steep angle toward the water surface. Where the two halves of the lower jaw meet at the front there is a toothlike or daggerlike bony projection, although it is not a real tooth. As this predator lunges at its prey (usually close to the water surface), it bends its head backward, thus increasing the gape of its already large mouth. Once the victim has been seized, the jaw is clamped shut and the prey prevented from escaping by the daggerlike "tooth."

0.4 inches (1.1 cm) standard length (the length from the tip of the snout to the base of the caudal fin). Adult *Danionella* are among the smallest freshwater vertebrates known to science. The lifespan of this transparent, scaleless little fish is estimated to be less than one year.

At the other extreme, sizewise, there are some very large American and Asian species. The largest Asian cyprinid is a carplike species from Cambodia and Thailand, *Catlocarpio siamensis*, which can grow to nearly 10 feet (3 m). It is said that when this fish is hooked, it can tow a fisherman's boat "for hours." Other Asian giants include the Tigris salmon (*Barbus esocinus*), which can reportedly grow to 7.6 feet (2.3 m) and a weight of 300 pounds (136 kg), the yellow cheek (*Elopichthys bambusa*) from the Amur River, which attains a length of

Mahseer (*Tor tor*)

Common name Mahseers

Scientific name *Tor* species

Family Cyprinidae

Subfamily Cyprininae

Order Cypriniformes

Size From around 2.1 in (5.3 cm) to around 9 ft (2.7 m)

Key features Body ranging from relatively slim to high backed; head with large eyes, no scales, and subterminal mouth; 2 pairs of fine barbels; lower lips fleshy; no lip teeth; body scales large in most species; few scales along the lateral line in most species with higher number in small-scaled species; well-formed fins; adipose fin absent; silvery coloration in most species; fins distinctly colored in some species, for example, deep-red pectorals, pelvics, and caudal fins in *T. sinensis*

Breeding Spawning generally late spring or early summer following an upriver migration; eggs generally scattered over gravel or pebbles and abandoned

Diet Wide range of food: large species may feed on fish, crustaceans, and other invertebrates; also plant material, including fruits and algae

Habitat Large, fast-flowing rivers with rocky or gravelly beds; a few species in smaller, slower streams and pools

Distribution Widely distributed in Asia: Afghanistan, India, Bangladesh, Pakistan, Nepal, China, Sri Lanka, Malay Peninsula, Borneo, Sumatra (Indonesia), Java, Thailand, Vietnam, and Laos

Status *Tor yunnanensis* officially listed as Endangered; now much more restricted in its distribution than formerly

⊕ *The mahseer (*Tor tor*), native to Asia, is often found in fast-flowing rivers. Length to 4.9 ft (1.5 m), mostly now less.*

Mahseers

Tor species

Mahseers resemble another group of cyprinids, the barbs. However, there is one distinct difference: Barbs are generally small fish measuring no more than a few inches, whereas the mahseers include species that grow to 9 feet (2.7 m) in length.

THE 15 CLOSELY RELATED SPECIES known as mahseers all have a scaleless head, no true lip teeth, no clearly demarcated stomach, and no adipose fin, although the other fins are well formed. Mahseers share these features with barbs, which are also grouped in the subfamily Cyprininae. Like most species of barb, especially some of the Indian species, mahseers also have large silvery scales, large eyes, and fine barbels around the mouth. It is probably these latter features, more than any others, that make mahseers appear like barbs.

In the case of at least one species, *Tor polylepis* from the Yunnan Province of China, the similarities go even further: Its length (as far as we know) is just 2.1 inches (5.3 cm)—comfortably within the size range of many of the barbs, such as the tiger barb (*Barbus [Puntius] tetrazona*) and its immediate relatives. In fact, the similarities and overlaps between mahseers and barbs are such that mahseers still sometimes appear in books under the scientific name of *Barbus*. Most modern texts, however, place them in their own genus, *Tor*.

The Giants

Most of the larger species of mahseer are considered as either food fish, game (sport) fish, or both. "The" mahseer (*T. tor*) is perhaps the most famous member of the genus, being highly regarded as a sporting fish. It can grow to 4.9 feet (1.5 m) and weigh around 150 pounds (68 kg), although most are smaller. The longest species is the putitor, or golden mahseer (*T. putitora*), which reaches 9 feet (2.7 m) and a weight of 120 pounds (54 kg). Both species occur in the Himalayas, with *T. tor* being found

⊕ *The Thai tor (*Tor tambroides*) is a popular food fish. However, because it feeds on toxic fruits at certain times of the year, it is not always a safe choice for human consumption.*

in Bangladesh, India, Pakistan, Nepal, and Bhutan, and *T. putitora* also in Afghanistan. According to some reports, the mahseer *T. tor* is the most common mahseer species; others, however, identify the putitor mahseer as the most abundant and most widely distributed.

The Thai mahseer (*T. tambroides*) grows to around 3.3 feet (1 m). It is distributed through the Malay Peninsula, Sumatra, Borneo, Java, and surrounding areas, where it is regarded as more of a food fish than as a game fish.

Tor tambra grows to a similar size and has a range distribution similar to the Thai mahseer, although it is not thought to be exploited in the same way as the Thai mahseer.

The heaviest species is the high-backed mahseer (*T. mussalah*) from India; while it only measures around 4.9 feet (1.5 m), it can weigh nearly 200 pounds (90 kg), making it a much

sought-after game fish. Despite its much smaller size of around 20 inches (50 cm), the Deccan mahseer (*T. khudree*) from central India and Sri Lanka is also considered a good game fish. Since its flesh is considered to be of medicinal value, this species is particularly sought after as a food fish.

Scale Cards

Mahseers have large body scales. The putitor, or golden mahseer, being the largest species, also has the largest scales. In the past the scales were used in a most unusual way. The species was first described by in 1822, when it was reported that the putitor "...is found nine feet in length, and six feet is the usual size. The scales are exceedingly large, being like the hand, and at Dacca are often made into the cards with which people game."

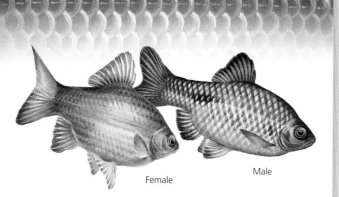

Female   Male

Rosy barb (*Barbus [Puntius] conchonius*)

Common name Barbs

Scientific name *Barbus* spp. (including *Capoëta*, *Puntius*, and *Barbodes*)

Family   Cyprinidae

Subfamily Cyprininae

Order   Cypriniformes

Number of species About 700

Size   From about 1.2 in (3 cm) to about 14 in (35 cm); most species under 4 in (10 cm)

Key features Most species have a laterally compressed body, being deepest (from top to bottom) in region of dorsal fin; head usually oval shaped and scaleless; 2–4 fine barbels around mouth; jaws can be extended forward when opened; dorsal fin located about halfway along back; anal fin small; well-formed caudal fin; lateral line runs along midline of body or slightly above it

Breeding   Sticky eggs scattered among plants or over the substratum and then abandoned; hatching may take 1 day but usually takes over 2 days

Diet   Plants, aquatic invertebrates, and insects; larger species also eat small fish

Habitat   Wide range of habitats from clear, flowing mountain rivers and streams to lowland water courses, ditches, canals, and flooded fields

Distribution *Barbus* found in Africa and Europe; *Capoëta* found in North Africa and the Near East; *Puntius* widely distributed in southern Asia; *Barbodes* mainly in Indonesia and Sulawesi

World population Abundant overall, but some species considered to be under threat

Status   At least 14 species listed as Critically Endangered, 4 Endangered, 1 Vulnerable, with list growing; 26 species of *Barbus* are considered under threat (see box "Endangered Barbs")

⬆ *The rosy barb (Barbus [Puntius] conchonius), native to Africa and Europe, is usually about 4 in (10 cm) in length and can be found in both fast and slow-moving waters.*

Barbs

Barbus species

Despite the popularity and abundance of barbs in fishkeeping circles, the World Conservation Union lists no fewer than 53 barb species as being at risk in the wild, mainly due to habitat pollution.

BETWEEN 1980 AND 1982 RANGIT Bandula paid regular visits to an unnamed stream on a rubber plantation in Sri Lanka. On each visit he was able to collect around 100 barbs per hour. Between 1989 and 1990 Rohan Pethiyagoda, a Sri Lankan scientist who visited the stream on five separate occasions, managed to collect a maximum of just 14 barbs. In seven to nine years the Bandula barb (*Barbus bandula*) had gone from being an abundant species to one on the brink of extinction.

Endangered Richness

Sri Lanka enjoys great riches in terms of freshwater and marine fish species. Many of them have been highly popular not only with scientists but also with aquarists the world over. Among the best known of the species are Sri Lanka's many barbs, some of which have been bred in captivity over many years and have been developed into a number of color and fin varieties.

Among those that have been bred commercially are the cherry barb (*B. titteya*), Cuming's barb (*B. cumingii*), and the black ruby barb (*B. nigrofasciatus*), all three of which are under threat in the wild. None, however, appears to be under such intense pressure as the Bandula barb.

Known since at least 1980, the Bandula barb has never been collected in any significant numbers. Almost certainly the greater accessibility of populations of similarly patterned species, allied to commercial breeding programs for the Bandula barb, have played a major role in reducing its decimation in the wild.

One of the key factors leading to the dramatic decline in numbers appears to be some form of repeated pollution, probably

The cherry barb (Barbus [Puntius] titteya) grows to a maximum of 1 inch (3 cm), and the males show maximum coloration during the breeding period. The female is a silvery pinkish color. Both sexes have in common a gold and black stripe down the side of the body.

consisting of runoff from the rice paddies that lie upstream of the original locality of the Bandula barb, as well as the rubber plantation through which the unnamed stream runs.

All is not gloom and doom, though. Some time after the collections for the official description of the species were made, a number of specimens were passed on to Ananda Pathirana, one of Sri Lanka's commercial ornamental fish breeders and exporters, who has succeeded in breeding several thousand specimens that could be released back into the

wild. Due to the threats to the original locality, efforts have been made to find a suitable alternative location. This has not proved an easy challenge, since alternative locations are always likely to have their own natural species, whose balance could be upset by the introduction of what could be termed an "exotic" species. Nevertheless, several potentially suitable locations were found in 2001–2002, and some controlled restocking was undertaken.

Despite this, the future of the Bandula barb in the wild is still poised on a knife edge: The

type population, in other words, the one found in the original locality, could be wiped out overnight if its native stream suffers a major pollution incident. Yet there are very few safe alternative locations in the whole of Sri Lanka into which either wild or captive-bred specimens can be released. One ray of hope, however, is that while efforts to ensure its continued survival in nature continue, stocks are still being built up gradually in the relative safety of an enterprising fish breeder's facilities.

The Bandula barb is not the only barb species whose survival is uncertain. Some, like the black ruby barb, the cherry barb, and Cuming's barb, are being monitored but face no immediate threat of extinction. Others, though, like the Asoka barb (*B. asoka*) and Martenstyn's barb (*B. martenstyni*), also from Sri Lanka, along with some 14 Philippine species, nine or more South African species, and several European species, all face serious threats. In total the World Conservation Union lists no fewer than 53 barb species as being of concern, including the unusual cave-dwelling African blind barb (*Caecobarbus geertsi*).

Barbus, Puntius, Barbodes...or Capoëta?

At some time or other anyone who tries to study barbs will be thrown into a state of confusion by the various scientific names used to refer to these species. The fact is that while it is easy to recognize a barb as a barb, knowing how to refer to it in scientific terms is fraught with ambiguities. In some countries, for example, all barbs are regarded as belonging to the genus *Barbus*, while the very same fish can appear under a variety of other names elsewhere. The same applies to scientists: Some, for example, may refer to the tiger barb as *Barbus tetrazona,* and others call it *Puntius tetrazona.* So, who is right?

There is no simple answer, which is hardly surprising when one considers how widely distributed these fish are. The various species of barbs are found throughout most of Africa, Sri Lanka, Europe, India, China, Indonesia, and a sizable part of Asia. They also form a highly variable group in terms of size, coloration, and behavior. For example, in size they range from nearly 40 inches (1.2 m) in length in the case of the European barbel (*Barbus barbus*), whereas at the other extreme the majority of species rarely exceed 3 inches (7.5 cm).

Repeated attempts have been made over the years to rationalize the classification of the barbs, but the result of this activity has often been yet more confusion. One radical attempt at classification was to group the three genera of barbs according to the number of barbels they had: *Barbus* species with four barbels, *Capoëta* species with two barbels, and *Puntius* species lacking barbels.

However convenient it would be for such subdivisions to be valid, barbel differences are not as clear-cut as they may seem at first sight. For example, it has been found that the number of barbels is not constant within a species; even individual broods from a single breeding pair can show variation in the number of barbels! So neither barbels nor any other single character, or combination of characters, is an infallible method of identification.

A major revision of the whole group is needed to help clarify the present confused state of affairs. Until this survey is completed, many authorities

⊕ The tiger barb (Barbus [Puntius] tetrazona), also known as the Sumatra barb, can grow to a length of 2 inches (5 cm). The black "tiger" stripes provide efficient camouflage by breaking up the shape of the fish as it swims among plant stems and the substrate.

(including Nelson, 1994) are choosing to maintain the status quo by regarding all barbs as members of the genus *Barbus*, while accepting the fact that four generic names may still be used when referring to barbs.

A growing number of scientists have therefore applied the four generic names as follows:

Barbus—used for African and European species, for example, the barbel (*Barbus barbus*).

Capoëta—restricted to North African and Near Eastern species, for example, the Siraz Baligi (*Capoëta pestai*).

Puntius—used for the generally small southern Asian species, for example, the tiger barb (*Puntius tetrazona*).

Barbodes—restricted to the largish silvery barbs and their relatives, mainly from Indonesia and Sulawesi,

"Loose" *Puntius* Barbs

Although many authorities now regard the barbs as consisting of at least four genera: *Barbus, Capoëta, Puntius,* and *Barbodes, Puntius* has sometimes been used as a sort of "dumping ground" for many species that do not fit into any of the other three genera. This is largely the result of a rather loose description of what actually constitutes a *Puntius* barb.

Basically, a barb qualifies as a *Puntius* species if it has the following features:
• Length 4 inches (10 cm) or smaller
• A robust body—despite being laterally compressed
• Small barbels with jaws that extend forward when spread, in other words, protrusible jaws
• A smooth, oval-shaped head
• A dorsal fin located more or less in the center of the back
• A short anal fin
• Two well-formed lobes in the caudal fin
• A lateral line organ running along the middle of the body or slightly above

The difficulty with these requirements is that more than 100 species of southern Asian barb also have the features. Therefore, some of the species currently regarded as *Puntius* species may eventually turn out to belong to another genus altogether.

⤒ *The tinfoil barb (Barbus [Barbodes] schwanenfeldii) is relatively large, growing up to 14 inches (35 cm), and is found mainly in the waters around Indonesia and Sulawesi.*

for example, the tinfoil barb (*Barbodes schwanenfeldii*).

In the following text all species will be referred to as *Barbus*. However, the alternative classification based on the different groups described above is also shown: for example, the tiger, or Sumatra, barb (*Barbus [Puntius] tetrazona*).

Banded Relatives

The tiger, or Sumatra, barb is one of the most easily identifiable of all the small Asian barbs. It has four bold black vertical bands on its body ("tetra" means four) superimposed on a light-colored base. The first band extends from the

→ *The golden tinfoil barb (*Poropuntius malcolmi*) is bred exclusively for use in aquariums.*

top of the head through the eye and down to the "throat" area. The second band is on the front half of the body, the third on the back half, and the fourth on the caudal peduncle (base of the tail). There are, however, some specimens that also have a black spot or blotch about halfway between the two body bands. Nevertheless, all are clearly tiger barbs.

Moving up the number scale, the five-banded barb has, as its name states, an additional black band. It is therefore known as *B. (P.) pentazona* ("penta" means five). Halfway between the tiger barb and the five-banded barb is another species that has four complete bands and a partially developed one. Not unnaturally, this barb is known as *B. (P.) partipentazona*.

The banded or striped barb is known as *B. (P.) johorensis* (it is found near Johore in Malaysia) and has the same number of bands as the five-banded barb, though they are much less pronounced. In the round-banded barb, known as *B. (P.) rhomboocelatus*, there are also (usually) five bands, but they are split in the center so they form an ocellus, or "eye," and they are quite faint compared with the bands that occur in the tiger barb and the five-banded barb. Finally, there is the six-banded, or hex, barb known as *B. (P.) hexazona* ("hexa" means six). In this barb the spaces between the bands are much smaller than in the tiger barb, and the bands themselves are much narrower.

All species (some scientists regard at least some as subspecies) are exceptionally attractive and represent an excellent example of the various permutations that are possible on the basic four-to-six-band theme.

Dwarves and Tinfoils

Within the genus *Barbus*—taken in the widest context—the largest species is the European barbel (*Barbus barbus*) of fresh waters, which can occasionally grow to around 40 inches (1.2 m) and a weight of 26.5 pounds (12 kg).

Enigmatic Odessas

Everyone who sets eyes on this barb agrees that by any standards, it is a beautiful fish. Few people, however, agree on its identity, except that most are of the opinion that the Odessa barb is not a naturally occurring species. In 1971–72 news broke that a new barb had been discovered in a fish bazaar in Odessa, Russia. Within a few years the new "species" had become popular and widespread, and was being bred in reasonable numbers. Despite this, its true identity remains a mystery. Indeed, the scientific name often given to this barb, *Barbus* "Odessa," is technically invalid.

The fact is that although there are several species of barb that look to a greater or lesser extent similar to the Odessa barb, no Odessas appear to have ever been found in the wild. Inevitably, therefore, this has led to the belief that the Odessa barb is not a true species at all but is more likely to have somehow arisen, by accident or design, from one or other of the following potential ancestral candidates: The ticto, or tic-tac-toe, barb (*B. [P.] ticto*)—regarded by some as a subspecies: *B. ticto ticto*; Stoliczk's barb (*B. [P.] stoliczkanus*—also referred to as *B. ticto stoliczkanus, B. stoliczkae,* or most recently as a naturally occurring form of the ticto barb; Cuming's barb (*B. [P.] cumingi*); or the rosy barb (*B. [P.] conchonius*). Some people believe the Odessa barb to be a color variety of the ticto barb, while others believe it to be the result of crosses between some of its presumed ancestral species.

Blind Discovery

In 1917 a team of cave explorers entered some 1,650 feet (500 m) into a cave situated about 3,300 feet (700 m) above sea level in the Lower Congo River system, Zaire. There they found a small, pink-colored, blind fish that had been reported two years earlier by a Belgian explorer, M. Delporte. After the First World War one member of the cave team, M. Geerts, took some specimens back to Belgium, where the species was officially described as *Caecobarbus geertsi* in his honor.

The Congo blind barb, or the blind cave barb, has since then been found at other localities, but all in the same region of the Lower Congo. It is believed to be rare and, owing to its restricted distribution, open to threat of extinction. The World Conservation Union has therefore officially classified *C. geertsi* as being Vulnerable, the category just below Endangered. It is also listed by the Convention in International Trade in Endangered Species (CITES) in its Appendix II, indicating that trade is strictly monitored and requires special permits.

However, within the narrower range that is made up of the species variously referred to by some scientists as *Barbodes*, *Capoëta*, and *Puntius*, the largest representatives are the tinfoil barb (*Barbus* [*Barbodes*] *schwanenfeldii*)—now reclassified by some scientists in a new genus, *Barbonymus*—and its relatives. Some mature specimens can grow to nearly 14 inches (35 cm) and are considered important food fish in their Asian home waters.

The tinfoil barb itself is also considered an important aquarium fish, despite its relatively large size and the fact that it forms shoals. Several varieties have therefore been produced by breeders exclusively for home aquariums.

At the bottom of the scale is the dwarf, or golden, barb—perhaps more accurately also known as the golden dwarf barb (B. [P.] gelius). This tiny barb is fully mature at 1.2 inches (3 cm) and grows to 1.6 inches (4 cm) at most. It is a very attractively marked species, having a silvery belly and bold black blotches on a shiny golden base that extends on to the head.

Another, larger species also known as the golden barb is, in fact, a golden form of the half-striped, Chinese, or green barb (B. [P.] semifasciolatus).

⊖ *The clown barb (Barbus [Puntius] everetti) has a cheerfully random coloration, with blotches of black occurring apparently indiscriminately on a gold, yellow, silver, and pinkish background. The clown barb can grow to 5 inches (13 cm) in length.*

Barbs under Threat

Critically Endangered Barbs
Twee River redfin (B. [B.] erubescens), border barb (B. [B.] trevelyani)—South Africa
petropsaro (B. [B.] euboicus)—Greece
pait (B. [P.] amarus), baoulan (B. [P.] baoulan), bagangan (B. [P.] clemensi), disa (B. [P.] disa), katapa-tapa (B. [P.] flavifuscus), B. [P.] herrei, katolo (B. [P.] katolo), kandar (B. [P.] lanaoensis), manalak (B. [P.] manalak), tras (B. [P.] tras)—Philippines
Bandula barb (B. [P.] bandula)—Sri Lanka

Endangered Barbs
Clanwilliam redfin (B. [B.] calidus), sailfin (B. [B.] serra)—South Africa
Asoka barb (B. [P.] asoka), Martenstyn's barb (B. [P.] martenstyni)—Sri Lanka

Vulnerable Barbs
blind cave barb (Caecobarbus geertsi)—Zaire

Other species from the above countries, as well as Spain, Portugal, Italy, Switzerland, Albania, Armenia, Azerbaijan, Georgia, Iran, Macedonia, Russia, Turkey, Ukraine, Bulgaria, Croatia, Slovenia, Mozambique, and Namibia are also under varying degrees of threat.

European Barbel

Barbus barbus

This is a powerful fish of fast-flowing waters, feeling for food on the bottom with the sensory barbels that give the species its common name.

Common name Barbel (European barbel)

Scientific name *Barbus barbus*

Family   Cyprinidae

Subfamily Cyprininae

Order   Cypriniformes

Size   Up to a maximum of 40 in (1.2 m) and weight of 26.5 lb (12 kg) but usually smaller

Key features Pointed snout; underslung mouth with 2 pairs of fleshy barbels; thick lips; scaleless head; smallish eyes set high on sides of head; elongated body, almost cylindrical in cross-section; back slightly curved, but belly flat; all fins well formed; adipose fin absent; greenish-brown coloration on back, turning to golden along the sides

Breeding   Spawning from late spring through summer, following short upstream migration to gravelly areas; up to 50,000 sticky, yellowish, poisonous eggs may be scattered over the bottom and abandoned; hatching takes 10–15 days

Diet   Bottom-living invertebrates (especially the larvae of two-winged insects), algae, and detritus; may also take small fish

Habitat   Flowing rivers with sandy or gravelly bottoms; also found in pools

Distribution From central and eastern England through France and eastward through Europe to Russia; absent from Scandinavia, Ireland, Denmark, and the Iberian Peninsula (populations present in Spain and Morocco are from introduced stocks)

THE POWER OF THIS FISH, coupled with its relatively large size, make it popular with sport fishermen who seek it out in fast-flowing rivers and weirs.

"Selective" Distribution

Although this species is called the European barbel, it is not native to every country in Europe. For example, it is absent from Italy, Spain, Portugal, and parts of Scandinavia such as Denmark.

Like many large cyprinid species such as carps, the barbel has been introduced into several locations outside its natural range, which extends from England eastward through Europe to Russia. Thus, for example, it was introduced into Lago Banyoles in Catalonia around 1910 and to Morocco from 1926.

Protective Colors

Barbel are bottom-dwelling fish with generally dull coloration. The fins visible from above—the dorsal, pectorals, and caudal—are dark, while the anal and pelvics, only visible from the side, are yellowish-orange. The sides of the body are much lighter than the back.

This coloration and patterning offers barbels two survival advantages: Since they tend to inhabit relatively deep water, they are difficult to spot from the air; from the side, though, they can make themselves visible to other members of the species.

Interestingly, juvenile specimens, which tend to inhabit areas of shallower water often with a gravelly or pebbly bottom, have irregular spotting on the body. This, too, acts as camouflage against attacks from kingfishers, herons, and other fish-eating birds.

Ⓓ *Well camouflaged from above, the European barbel combs the riverbed for food with its barbel sensors.*

Genetic Double Act

Most fish have their genetic information—the codes that determine everything from shape, color, and even behavior—contained in about 50 tiny structures called chromosomes found in their cell nuclei (see Glossary). At some stage during barbel evolution a fundamental change occurred, as a result of which the number of chromosomes was doubled to 100. This means that each nucleus contains twice as much genetic material.

The doubling of the chromosome number has also been found in two of the European barbel's closest relatives, the Mediterranean, or southern, barbel (*B. meridionalis*), from southern France, northern Spain, Italy, and parts of the Danube basin, and the Po barbel (*B. plebejus*), from Italy, Dalmatia, and Sicily.

Chromosome doubling also occurs in the goldfish (*Carassius auratus auratus*).

Other European Barbels

Although *B. barbus* is known as the European barbel, it is not the only European species in the genus—although it is the only one found in the British Isles. As well as the southern or Mediterranean barbel and the Po barbel there are also several other European species.

The Greek barbel (*B. graecus*) is found in only two lakes: Paralimni and Yliki; it is also found in the Sperchios River. The Euboean barbel, or Petropsaro (*B. euboicus*), is also Greek. It occurs only on the island of Euboea and is listed by the World Conservation Union as Critically Endangered. *Barbus albanicus* is native to Greece and Albania, hence its name. *B. caninus* is found in Italy and Switzerland, while the Turkish, or Thracian, barbel (*B. cyclolepis*) is found not just in Turkey but in surrounding countries as well. The Caucasian barbel (*B. ciscaucasicus*) occurs in the rivers flowing into the Caspian Sea.

The Caspian barbel (*B. brachycephalus*) is unusual not only for its size (up to a maximum of 3.9 feet /1.2 m), but because it occurs in salt water in the Caspian and Aral Seas.

Other European species include the Peloponnesian barbel (*B. peloponnesius*), the Briána (*B. prespensis*) from Albania, Greece, and Macedonia, *B. sclateri* from Portugal and Spain, and *B. tyberinus* from Italy.

Under Threat

The Iberian barbel (*B. comizo*), *B. microcephalus*, from Spain and Portugal, the Mediterranean barbel (*B. guiraonis*), the red-tailed barbel (*B. haasi*), both from Spain, and *B. steindachneri*, from Portugal, are officially listed as Vulnerable. There is, however, a second Iberian barbel (*B. bocagei*), subdivided into several subspecies, which is not on the official World Conservation Union Red List.

Common Carp

Cyprinus carpio carpio

Carp can be extremely longlived fish. The maximum recorded age for a common carp is 47 years.

THE COMMON CARP IS A LARGE, heavy-bodied fish that originated in Central Asia, east of the Caspian Sea. From there, it spread eastward into the Manchurian region of China during the later glaciations of the Ice Age. Then it began spreading naturally westward to the Danube basin and the Black and Aral Seas.

This species is probably the first fish to have been introduced outside its native range by humans. The Romans may have been the first to begin the process, with fish being removed from the Danube and released elsewhere in Europe during the 1st to 4th centuries AD. The fish were usually introduced and cultured for human consumption.

The pace of introductions was irregular for many centuries but picked up during the 20th century, to the extent that the common carp in its various forms is now found virtually throughout the world, except where environmental conditions are too severe for it. This "redistribution" has been so thorough, and the species is found in such numbers, especially throughout Europe, that many people believe the common carp to be a true European fish despite its Central Asian origins.

In many places where the species now occurs, it is exploited as a food or a sport fish. In some countries, though, it is considered a pest, and attempts are repeatedly being made to eliminate it. The fact is that although the common carp is peaceful and tolerant, it can cause great disturbance in its "adopted" range, particularly where large specimens are present in some numbers. A serious potential consequence is that local species of plants and animals can be inadvertently placed under threat of extinction by this inoffensive fish.

⊖ *Three varieties of common carp: mirror carp (top); common carp (center); leather carp (bottom).*

Common name Common carp (European carp, koi)

Scientific name *Cyprinus carpio carpio*; there are also several naturally occurring varieties regarded as subspecies

Family Cyprinidae

Subfamily Cyprininae

Order Cypriniformes

Size Up to around 4 ft (1.2 m) or more in length and a weight of around 82 lb (37.3 kg) but usually smaller

Key features Heavy-bodied fish; fully scaled body; scaleless head with underslung mouth bearing 2 pairs of barbels; well-formed fins; coloration variable but usually greenish-brown on back fading to yellowish-creamish along belly; ornamental varieties exhibit wide range of colors

Breeding Season extends from spring into summer; over 1,660,000 sticky eggs scattered among vegetation in shallow water; no parental care; hatching takes 5–8 days

Diet Wide-ranging, including vegetation, bottom-living invertebrates, and insects

Habitat Wide range of habitats, particularly larger, slow-flowing or still bodies of water; can tolerate some salt in water; preferred temperature range 37–95° F (3–35° C)

Distribution From its initial central Asian origins the species is now found almost worldwide

Status Although the species *C. carpio* is under no threat of extinction, some populations in a number of countries, for example Austria, Hungary, and Romania, are regarded as Critically Endangered; main causes are decreases in range and decline in habitat quality caused by pollutants and other environmental factors

↑ *Common carp feed at various levels in the water, from the muddy bottom to the surface.*

Common Carp Splits

Mainly due perhaps to the extremely wide distribution of the common carp, the genus *Cyprinus* is often regarded as being highly variable, and wrongly as monotypic—in other words, containing a single species: *Cyprinus carpio*. In fact, the genus also contains other, lesser known and less widely distributed representatives (see later).

Cyprinus carpio is widely known in three quite different forms:

• The "basic" wild type, which is fully scaled and is usually called the common carp;

• A scaleless, or naked type, the leather carp;

• An almost scaleless type with a few rows of large, reflective scales, called the mirror carp.

In addition, over many years the above

characteristics have been bred into ornamental varieties—known as koi—giving rise to some amazing combinations of color and body type. Despite the modifications that all the derived forms have, there are still some common carp characteristics that we can detect in the cultivated descendants, including koi. Among them are a body length of up to 40 inches (1 m) or more, four barbels (two on each side, on the upper lip and the corners of the mouth), and a dorsal fin with a long base. The dorsal fin stretches over a considerable part of the back of the fish. It contains 17 to 22 branched rays, preceded by a strong, toothed spine.

Traditionally, all the cultivated forms have been regarded as varieties of the single species *C. carpio,* or common carp. However, during

the 1990s various studies resulted in the species being subdivided into four subspecies. The common carp is therefore now *C. carpio carpio*, so all the above are now regarded as varieties of this subspecies.

A second subspecies, the Amur carp (*C. carpio haematopterus*) from the Amur basin and surrounding regions, is very similar to the common carp. Like the common carp, it is exploited commercially. However, there are several fin and gill differences that separate it from the common carp; it is also the most resistant of all four subspecies to low temperatures.

Differences in the number of vertebrae (back bones), the number of scales in the lateral line, and in the gill rakers (see Glossary) also separate *C. carpio viridiviolaceus* from Vietnam and southern China from its closest relatives. The fourth subspecies, *C. carpio chilia*, is known from most of the lakes on the Yunnan Plateau in China. However, little detailed data is available on this subspecies.

⊕ *A common carp feeding on the bottom using its sensory barbels to detect food. Once food is located, it is sucked into the huge mouth.*

Common Carp Cousins

In addition to splitting the common carp species into four subspecies, a number of reviews of the genus carried out during the 1980s and 1990s resulted in its reorganization into no fewer than 14 species (including *C. carpio*). Some, like the common carp itself, are fished commercially, even though they may be small in size, for example, *C. acutidorsalis*, which is found in river mouths in Asia, and *C. multi-taeniata* (whose name means "many-striped"), which only occurs in the West River in China. Others are equally, or even more, restricted in their distribution, for example, *C. barbatus*, *C. daliensis,* and *C. longipectoralis*, all of which are only known from Lake Erchai in the Mekong River basin in Yunnan Province, China, or *C. ilishaetomus* from Lake Qiluhu, also in Yunnan. Yet others have descriptive names, such as *C. megalophthalmus*, meaning "large eye," while one, *C. pellegrini*, is a specialized feeder, its diet consisting of plankton.

Two members of the genus are included by the World Conservation Union in its Red List of threatened species. *Cyprinus micristius*, which occurs only in Lake Dian Chi in Yunnan, China, is considered to be Endangered, mainly due to its extremely restricted distribution in the lake, while *C. yilongensis*, known only from Lake Yi-lung (again, in Yunnan Province, China), is now believed to be extinct.

Fish of Many Names

The wide distribution of the common carp (both natural and introduced), plus its natural tendency to vary according to location and environmental conditions, has led to numerous scientific descriptions of "new" species over the years. In total there have been around 74 such descriptions since the original one made in 1758. Gradually, over the years all the descriptions have been reexamined, with the result that 49 have been found to refer to just one species, *Cyprinus carpio*. Further study has resulted in *C. carpio* being split into four subspecies.

Other revisions, and more recent and more accurate descriptions, have meant that the common carp genus, *Cyprinus*, has been narrowed down to 14 species and four subspecies. Only two have common names: the common carp (*C. carpio carpio*) and the Amur carp (*C. carpio haematopterus*). The full listing is: *C. carpio carpio*, *C. carpio haematopterus*, *C. carpio chilia*, *C. carpio viridiviolaceus*, *C. acutidorsalis*, *C. barbatus*, *C. daliensis*, *C. ilishaestomus*, *C. intha*, *C. longipectoralis*, *C. mahuensis*, *C. megalophthalmus*, *C. micristius*, *C. multitaeniata*, *C. pellegrini*, *C. yilongensis*, *C. yunnanensis.*

Little detailed information is available on the three remaining species: *C. intha* from Southeast Asia, *C. mahuensis* from Ma-Hu in Szechwan, China, and *C. yunnanensis*, yet another *Cyprinus* species from Yunnan.

Culinary Carp

In addition to their great popularity as game or sport fish the various cultivated forms of the common carp (except koi) are also in great demand for the table. In fact, so-called "table" carp have been reared specifically for human consumption ever since the Romans began their program of carp introductions.

This tradition was subsequently adopted by European monks who found in the carp a fish that grew rapidly on a wide range of foods, was hardy, delicious to eat, and the perfect alternative to meat on days of abstinence, such as Friday, when meat eating was not allowed.

Many monasteries built their own carp ponds, some of which were so robust and well designed that they are still operational today. Pond carp culture soon became so vital to monasteries that a great deal of time and effort went into improving culture techniques, methods of collecting fish easily, and so on. Many water engineering innovations, some of which are still in existence today, were devised by monks. One of them, the sluice—the gate and channel arrangement used for regulating water flow and for controlling the drainage of ponds—is actually known as a "monk."

In eastern Europe especially, carp forms an essential part of the family menu, particularly on important days. Many eastern European families therefore eat carp at Christmas instead of indulging in the more western habit of eating turkey.

Numerous recipes are available, many

⌖ Despite appearances, this common carp is not stranded but is spawning in shallow water.

Reading the Rings

It is possible to roughly calculate the age of a fish by counting the growth rings in the bones known as otoliths or ear stones. This is similar to the method of calculating the age of trees by counting the growth rings in the trunk. However, unlike a tree, in which a new growth ring is produced every year, the difficulty in using growth ring counts as a way of estimating the age of a fish is that the information can be easily misread. A fish does not simply lay down one growth ring each year; the growth rings are influenced by many factors such as the health of the fish, the kind of habitat it lives in, and the availability of food.

Periods of active growth, when new tissues are being created at a rapid rate, are reflected in the bones. In the case of the otoliths rapid growth results in a light-colored ring of calcium carbonate being laid down. So, since spring and summer are generally the seasons of fastest growth, the period is represented in each otolith as a relatively wide, light-colored zone. Then, as growth slows down during fall and eventually stops altogether during the coldest part of the year, the ring becomes narrower, denser, and darker. In the following spring the cycle begins again.

If a fish remains healthy, finds plenty of food, and does not live in a polluted environment, then growth and no-growth periods will alternate without disruption. In such cases the otoliths will show this in the form of a light-colored, broader ring surrounded by a thinner, darker one produced every year. But if growth stops or is checked during the normal growing season, the fish will not be able to continue laying down its light-colored ring. Instead, it will be forced into the darker-ring phase. As a result, there will be two light and dark rings laid that year. If, instead of one or two, there are several growth interruptions, they will also be reflected in the number of light and dark rings laid down. The longer a fish survives, the greater the likelihood it will experience situations that disrupt its normal growth patterns. Therefore, if an otolith shows, say, 50 rings, it is almost certain that the fish is actually considerably younger than 50 years old.

Applying this knowledge to a famous fish that was once believed to be 223 years old because she had that number of rings, it has now been estimated that the specimen in question (a large female koi known as Hanako) was not this age when she died but much younger. In fact, it is now believed that while ages of 40 to 50 years are quite achievable by carp in ideal conditions, anything in excess of 100 years must be regarded as "overoptimistic."

having been passed down from generation to generation, especially some of the more basic and wholesome ones like baked carp. Over time, though, as eastern Europeans have settled in other countries, carp eating has spread westward and, along with it, so has the demand for table carp. Recipes have become more westernized, too, with dishes like "Carp Farcie" and "Carpe à la Maitre d'Hotel" now rubbing shoulders with more traditional ones.

Prolific Breeder

In the wild the common carp likes quiet weedy waters, warm conditions (despite its hardiness), and a substratum in which it can root around for its wide-ranging diet of small creatures and vegetation. It can also withstand low levels of dissolved oxygen in the water.

Breeding occurs throughout summer, depending on actual location, in temperatures around 73° F (23° C), with the eggs being scattered among fine-leaved vegetation in shallow water. Spawning is a vigorous and sometimes violent affair, during which individuals may be injured. The results of such encounters (loss of scales, skin wounds, and so on) are usually relatively superficial and tend to heal of their own accord in healthy specimens.

The eggs (which can number many hundreds of thousands from a large female) hatch in five to eight days at around 73° F (23° C); the fry become free swimming several days later. Although many factors, like diet and state of health, can affect the total number of eggs that a female produces, a fairly accurate approximation is 100,000 per 2.2 pounds (1 kg) of body weight. Spawnings of well over a quarter of a million eggs are therefore quite commonplace not just in the common carp but in all its cultivated forms as well.

A female measuring as little as 18.5 inches (47 cm), for example, has been found to produce 300,000 eggs in a single spawning. Bearing in mind that adult females can often measure more than twice this length—nearly four feet (1.2 m)—and weigh around 82 pounds (37.3 kg), the species is to say the least highly prolific in the number of offspring it can potentially produce.

Koi Origins

Although nishikigoi—koi for short—have only been with us for something over 200 years, these majestic fish have been developed into so many configurations in this relatively short period that it is easy to lose sight of what,

biologically speaking, a koi, or brocaded carp, actually is. In fact, koi, like the common carp, are members of the species *Cyprinus carpio*. Looking at today's numerous and spectacular koi varieties, it is perhaps difficult to believe that they are all descended from what some describe as a dull, drab, and boring fish.

The first fish that could be genuinely regarded as ornamental varieties of common

The ornamental koi show a much more garish coloration than the wild species but share the same sleek lines and well-formed fins.

carp were developed in the Niigata Prefecture of Japan during the early part of the 19th century. The three main colors usually reported for the early koi are red, white, and yellow.

It is probably the case that these colored fish, which were subsequently bred into other forms, originally arose purely accidentally as the result of spontaneous mutations affecting the color genes in wild common carp stocks. There are accounts of colored carp (red and gray) from an earlier period (around 530 BC); but since these Chinese fish were almost certainly only regarded as food fish, it would be misleading to consider them as geniune koi.

From the early Japanese mutations numerous colorful and attractive varieties have been developed over the years, to the point that today virtually every pond owner will want

to own some of these large, glorious fish at some stage. Even up to the mid-1980s koi keeping tended to be regarded as a rather exclusive end of the pond hobby, basically because the fish were so expensive. Many potential owners were also put off by the names used to refer to the different varieties. It seemed to some as if you needed to learn Japanese before you could attempt to keep koi!

Things have changed dramatically since then. Although Japan still leads the world in the production of top koi bloodlines, other countries, like the U.S., Israel, and Britain, along with fish-producing regions like the Far East, are now producing numbers of koi as well.

Some of these fish may sometimes be less pure in terms of pedigree than those from a long-established Japanese bloodline, but they are colorful and every bit as robust. And they are considerably less expensive than pedigree stock. There is also now a wider variety of competitively priced Japanese koi available.

The result of these changes is that koi keeping has become much more accessible for the general pondkeeper, and this, in turn, has led to a massive surge in interest in these fish from pond owners who would not have considered keeping them in the past. Koi keeping is now an almost worldwide hobby.

Today's koikeepers span a wide-ranging spectrum, from those who are perfectly happy to own purely nonpedigree fish as long as they are attractive and healthy, to those specialists who only keep pedigree koi, or even pedigree specimens of just one variety of koi like the red and white kohaku. Most koikeepers, though, prefer a mixture of fish.

Koi Classification

Koi are classified according to their color, pattern of markings, and type of scales. Within these three broad criteria there are numerous permutations, resulting in well over 100 recognized varieties.

Colors, for instance, are referred to by the appropriate Japanese word; for example, *hi* (red), *sumi* (black), *ki* (yellow), and so on.

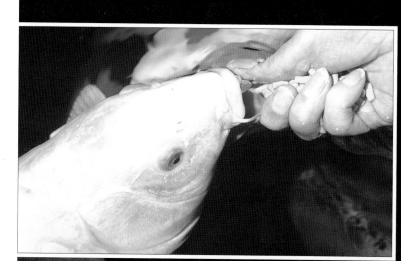

⊙ *Tame koi being hand fed. The koi can exert a powerful suck with its toothless mouth to take in food, which is then ground up by the pharyngeal teeth.*

Therefore, when referring to a fish in which the red markings are particularly good, one would say that its *hi* is of good quality.

Patterns are also referred to in Japanese. For example, a "lightning" or zig-zag pattern is referred to as *inazuma* patterning, while a *tancho* pattern tells us that the fish in question has a red patch in the center of the head. Scalation (the covering of scales on the body) can be complete, in which case it is said to be metallic, or restricted (or almost absent), in which case it is nonmetallic, as in leather and mirror carp, the mirror carp type being referred to as *doitsu* scaling. Other types of scalation can include highly reflective or sparkling patterns (known as *kinginrin* or *ginrin*), or scales that are rather small, revealing the skin in between (called *fucarin* scalation).

When other factors such as overall body coloring are also taken into consideration, it is not surprising, therefore, that a series of major categories, with innumerable subcategories, has been developed over the years for koi.

Mystery "Teeth"

Koi and other carpkeepers occasionally find unusual objects lying on the bottom of their pools. The objects look a little like teeth, but instead of being pointed, they are small, rounded cubes or three-dimensional rectangular structures, some with wrinkles on one of the surfaces. What can the objects be? The answer is that they are pharyngeal teeth, normally located in the throat and used for grinding food particles. Pharyngeal teeth can sometimes become dislodged, and then they are either swallowed or spit out. Either way, they eventually end up on the bottom of the pool.

⊙ *As its name suggests, the gold ghost koi is a rich golden color. Nevertheless, like other koi, it is still very much a carp. Even ornamental varieties still retain the typical carplike body shape.*

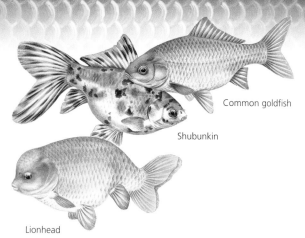
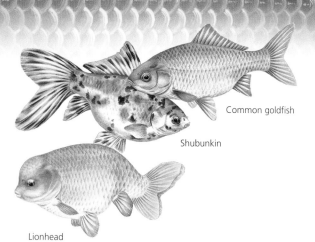

Common goldfish

Shubunkin

Lionhead

Some varieties of ornamental goldfish

Common name Goldfish (throughout the world); edible goldfish (Malaysia); gibel carp (Kazakhstan); gold crucian carp (Taiwan); golden carp and native carp (Australia)

Scientific name *Carassius auratus auratus*

Family Cyprinidae

Subfamily Cyprininae

Order Cypriniformes

Size Maximum length 23.2 in (59 cm); usually considerably smaller and lighter

Key features Robust, fully scaled body with scaleless head, which is roughly triangular in outline; dorsal fin with 3–4 spines and 15–19 soft rays; anal fin with 2–3 spines and 4–7 soft rays; all fins well formed; no barbels; range of colors—mainly olive-brown to olive-green, but grays, silvers, yellows, golds (with or without blotches), and others also known in wild populations; ornamental varieties exhibit a wide range of colors, finnage, and body shapes

Breeding Many thousands of sticky eggs produced and scattered among vegetation between spring and summer; hatching can take up to 1 week depending on temperature; breeding may involve gynogenesis (stimulation of egg development without fertilization taking place)

Diet Wide-ranging menu, including vegetation and small invertebrates

Habitat Found in a wide range of waters, including lakes, rivers, and ditches; still or slow-flowing waters are preferred, particularly those with soft sediments on the bottom

Distribution Originally from Central Asia, China, and Japan, but introduced virtually throughout the world

Goldfish

Carassius auratus auratus

The goldfish is one of the best-known animals in the world. As well as being the most popular aquarium fish, it is also by far the most popular and common of all pets.

ALMOST EVERYONE KNOWS THE GOLDFISH, and countless people have kept this delightful, colorful, and peaceful species. Numerous children have also been introduced to the world of fishkeeping by winning a fairground goldfish. (Happily, the practice of giving away a goldfish as a prize is now banned in many countries and is fast disappearing in others.)

To many fish lovers a typical goldfish is, as the name suggests, an active, gold-colored fish that is about 2 inches (5 cm) long and has a simple, streamlined body shape with large, friendly looking eyes. Constantly opening and closing its mouth, it is a fish that appears to be drinking water all the time. The goldfish also shows an endearing and immediate response to its owner once it learns to recognize him or her.

In fact, the common goldfish that everyone knows is, despite its basic finnage and body shape, already at least one step removed from the "real" goldfish, because any development or amplification of finnage, body color, or pattern signifies a step away from the wild form.

The natural coloration of the wild goldfish is commonly referred to as olive-brown. The crucial thing is that the color is not gold or orange-red. These and other colors may, nevertheless, be found in populations in some lowland river locations, small lakes, and backwaters in nature, but appear to be the result of introductions of domesticated varieties rather than true, wild fish.

Closest Relatives

The goldfish has a number of close relatives, the two closest probably being the gibel, or Prussian, carp (*C. gibelius*) and the crucian, or

⊕ The common and much-loved goldfish is not naturally gold in its wild state, and any wild fish that are gold probably descend from aquarium-bred varieties.

bronze, carp (*C. carassius*). In fact, the goldfish and the gibel carp were once believed to be a subspecies of *C. auratus*.

The goldfish is native to China and certain parts of Siberia, while the gibel carp, although also found in the wild in parts of Siberia (the west), is mainly an eastern European fish. In truly wild specimens the two species can be told apart by slight anatomical differences such as the size of the head relative to the body, the numbers of gill rakers (the spiny or comblike structures found on the gill arches that help filter out food from the water), fin rays, and scale counts. However, the virtually worldwide introduction of the goldfish into numerous natural bodies of water often clouds the true

distribution and nature of many of the populations found in the wild.

Species or Subspecies?

When the gibel, or Prussian, carp became recognized as a full species in its own right, in other words, as *C. gibelius* instead of *C. auratus gibelius*, most people then assumed that the goldfish, too, was now a full species, in other words, *C. auratus* instead of *C. auratus auratus*.

However, it is not quite as straightforward as this, since there are several fish that are very similar to the goldfish but are not quite the same. Yet they are all as different from the gibel, or Prussian, carp as the goldfish is. In addition, there is one other "goldfish-type" fish

Goldfish and Relatives

Scientific Name	*Carassius auratus auratus*
Common Name	Common goldfish
Approx. Size	12 inches (30 cm)
Dorsal Fin Outline	Straight to concave
Dorsal Fin Branched Rays	15–19
Lateral Line Scale Count	27–31
No. Gill Rakers	35–46

Scientific Name	*Carassius gibelius*
Common Name	Gibel carp; Prussian carp
Approx. Size	14.5 inches (36 cm)
Dorsal Fin Outline	Straight
Dorsal Fin Branched Rays	15–18
Lateral Line Scale Count	28–32
No. Gill Rakers	39–50

Scientific Name	*Carassius carassius*
Common Name	Crucian carp, bronze carp
Approx. Size	20 inches (50 cm)
Dorsal Fin Outline	Convex
Dorsal Fin Branched Rays	14–21
Lateral Line Scale Count	31–36
No. Gill Rakers	26–31

distinguish between different types, especially when they share many characteristics, that even the original describer of the goldfish ended up with no fewer than five new "species" and "subspecies" in the same year!

This process continued on and off until 1945, by which time there were 42 different official descriptions of the goldfish and goldfish-type fish. Since then they have been systematically studied, new findings have been added, and the whole group reassessed. As a result, the 42 "species" and "subspecies" have been reduced to just four species, one of which, the goldfish (*C. auratus*), is subdivided into four subspecies.

The full listing is: *C. auratus auratus* (goldfish; kin-buna*), *C. auratus buergeri* (naga-buna*), *C. auratus grandoculis* (nigoro-buna*), *C. auratus langsdorfii* (gin-buna*), *C. carassius* (crucian carp), *C. cuvieri* (gengorô-buna*), *C. gibelius* (gibel, or Prussian, carp).

Note: Names indicated by an asterisk (*) are the Japanese names for the fish. With the exception of the goldfish, all the others have almost exclusively Japanese distribution (*C. cuvieri* is also found in Taiwan and China, but only as a result of being introduced into these areas) and are little known outside Japan.

Genetic Manipulators

When the breeding season arrives, male goldfish develop small pimplelike growths, known as nuptial or breeding tubercles, on the snout, cheeks, gill covers, front edge of the pectoral fins, and sometimes, on top of the head and along the back. The tubercles are not unique to the goldfish or other cyprinids, but they are only found in males.

Owing to their rough texture, nuptial tubercles may help breeding (and slippery) fish maintain close body contact with each other during the actual act of spawning. This appears to be mostly the case with the cheek and pectoral fin tubercles, while those on the snout may also help stimulate females during spawning or repel rival males. Once the breeding season is over, the tubercles disappear,

that is not quite so similar, adding further to the challenges facing those whose responsibility it is to describe, separate, and group species and subspecies.

The position is similar to that of the common carp (*Cyprinus carpio carpio*) and its relatives. As if to emphasize the similarities, the goldfish was first scientifically described in 1758, the same year as the common carp, and by the same scientist, Linnaeus.

Again, as with the common carp, the wide distribution of the goldfish, along with its in-built "plasticity," which results in slightly different forms depending on location and conditions, has resulted in numerous "species" and "subspecies" being described over the years. In fact, it is sometimes so difficult to

although some roughened skin may remain in fully mature goldfish males.

Being able to perform the mating act successfully and producing offspring are two very different things, though. In other words, successful mating does not necessarily result in fertilized eggs. For this to happen, certain conditions have to be met, the most important being that the genetic content of the males' sperm must be able to fuse with the genetic content of the females' eggs.

Genetic information is contained in a number of tiny structures called chromosomes found in the nuclei of cells. Each species has a fixed number of these chromosomes, for example, 50. When sperm and eggs are produced, the number is halved, so that each sperm contains 25 chromosomes, and each egg contains 25 chromosomes. When successful mating occurs, the 25 sperm chromosomes pair up (fuse) with the 25 egg chromosomes, thus once more producing the original 50 chromosomes typical for the species.

↑ Bubble-eye goldfish demonstrate the fluid-filled sacs that protrude from their eye sockets. The sacs are delicate and liable to be punctured by sharp objects or other fish, leading to possible infection.

↪ Male goldfish develop breeding tubercles consisting of small growths that appear on various parts of the body, including the gill covers, pectoral fin edges, and front part of the head.

Genetically speaking, goldfish are fairly unusual because some can contain twice, three times, or even four times the usual number of chromosomes for the species. Therefore, while the basic number for the goldfish was originally 50, there are individuals with 100, 150, and 200 chromosomes.

This, of course, presents a major hurdle at

breeding time since, for example, the chromosomes within the sperm of a "100" male goldfish would find it impossible to pair up exactly with the chromosomes of a "150" or a "200" female.

Quite clearly, unless this genetic stumbling block is overcome, breeding is out of the question. Yet the mere fact that there are countless goldfish all over the world and that the species has been highly successful throughout its existence is living proof that the challenge has long been overcome. But how?

The solution lies in a process known as gynogenesis. When mating occurs, sperm enter eggs in the normal way. However, the genetic contents of the sperm and eggs do not fuse as would normally be the case. In fact, as we have seen, this would often be impossible. Instead, the sperm stimulate the eggs to begin developing without fusion actually taking place. Interestingly, since the eggs of "150" and "200" females are unable to go through the normal process in which their chromosome

number is halved, they already have the "full" number of chromosomes anyway. What we end up with, as a result, are clones, or exact replicas, of these females. Offspring produced in this way are therefore all females.

So where do males come from? They come from the "100" type whose chromosomes are capable of being halved, making it possible for "100" type males and females to breed in the normal way. Equally fascinating is that since the sperm do not fuse with the eggs but merely get development started, the sperm does not even have to come from a goldfish! Other closely related species will do just as well, including common carp (*Cyprinus carpio carpio*), rudds (*Scardinius* species), breams (*Abramis* species), and tench (*Tinca tinca*).

Chinese Origins
Tracing the history of any fish is fraught with difficulties. Details of experiments, chance observations, and other forms of documentation often prove impossible to find.

The calico fantail is an attractive ornamental variety with highly modified body shape, finnage, and coloration.

It will therefore come as no surprise to learn that the history of the goldfish, which spans more than 1,000 years, is strewn with complications, speculations, and other distracting elements. At times it is even difficult to tell fact from fiction. However, the story is all the more interesting precisely because of the uncertainties.

It is reported that several red-scaled fish were first observed some time between 265 and 316 AD, during the ancient Chinese Tsin Dynasty. If this is true, then the first steps toward the development of cultivated goldfish varieties had already been taken between around 1,500 and 1,700 years ago. However, there seems to be no absolutely firm evidence.

The first real piece of documented evidence we have comes from the Sung Dynasty of China (960–1279 AD), with records of goldfish kept as pets in ponds. At some stage during this period there was also a "goldfish pool" in Peking (now Beijing) where fish were bred commercially. Variously colored varieties, including combinations of gold, silver, red, black, and mottled forms, were already in existence by 1276. By the time the Ming Dynasty (1369–1644) was fully established, large numbers of these colored fish were being kept in aquariums made from clay.

Although selective breeding must have resulted in many combinations of color, finnage, and body shape, there is a gap of around 300 years before we have the first recorded example of a twin-tailed variety. In about 1590 a fantail was reported, followed in 1621 by transparent-scaled varieties.

Although experimentation must have been carried out continuously all this time, the next major recorded event is the appearance in 1726 of a variety totally lacking a dorsal fin. Since the evidence for it consists of a picture in the Chinese Imperial Encyclopedia, *T'u Shu*, it is reasonable to assume that the variety had already been in existence for some years prior to the publication of the encyclopedia.

This important document also includes illustrations of other fish without dorsal fins,

⊕ A red-eyed lionhead can be distinguished not only by its bulbous head and obvious red eyes but also by the absence of a dorsal fin—traces of which still remain in poorer quality specimens.

with upturned eyes, and with short, fat, oval bodies. All this can be taken as strong evidence, barring extreme artistic license, that the foundations for many of the later varieties had already been laid.

Japanese and Later Influences

Although by 1500 the goldfish had already been imported into Japan, it seems to have taken nearly 200 years for breeding experiments to expand into a major activity. The first known commercial enterprise is a breeding establishment set up by Sato Sanzaemon in Koriyama between 1704 and 1710.

Since then, however, Japan has played a major role in the development of numerous fancy goldfish (in other words, goldfish that carry modifications not found in the basic forms) from the few varieties—probably no more than five—that were originally imported from China. Although the list is long, the best-known varieties are undoubtedly the lionhead and the shubunkin. Yet even here there are

signs of some Chinese influence. This is confirmed by the fact that a "lionheadlike" fish is included in a series of drawings from China dating from around 1429.

Away from Japan the goldfish had become widespread in the Far East by the end of the 17th century. However, little or no selective breeding seems to have taken place here. By the middle of the 17th century the goldfish was well established in England and had been introduced into France, Italy, Germany, and the Netherlands. Scandinavia and Russia received specimens at the beginning and end of the 18th century respectively.

In America the first major importation took place in the mid-1870s, although some specimens may well have been seen there earlier. The person usually accredited the honor of introducing the goldfish to the American continent is Admiral Ammon, who is reported to have obtained his fish from Japan. There is some evidence, though, that the goldfish arrived in the U.S. before this date, but the original importation was never officially recorded.

The black moor in the color that might be expected from its name. Other colors, however, can be found under the moor variety. Note the double tail and protruding eyes.

Evolution in the Fast Lane

Evolution goes on very slowly most of the time. However, if we separate a small group of animals or plants from the rest of the species, this group or population can no longer interbreed with the rest of its kind. Under such conditions any characteristics the individuals in this small population might tend to have stand a better chance of becoming established, and of doing so much more rapidly, than if they were part of a larger breeding group.

This is what happened on the islands in the Galapagos Archipelago: They became geographically separated from the South American continent, and their fauna and flora developed in isolation, resulting in unique forms of finches, other birds, iguanas (lizards), and tortoises. If on top of the process of natural selection we add another factor, artificial selection, whereby humans choose which animals or plants are going to breed, the rate of change becomes even faster.

So it is with the goldfish, to the extent that today we have well over one hundred varieties of *C. auratus auratus*. They reflect variations such as modifications to the head (including the nostrils and eyes), the shape of the body, the shape, length—and even the presence or absence—of the fins, general coloration and patterning, the nature of the scales, and so on. Further, since one or more of the characteristics can occur in any combination, the resulting forms that can arise are virtually unlimited.

Ordering the Chaos

Making sense of the bewildering range of colors, shapes, sizes, finnage, scales, and so on is quite difficult, of course. However, there are some sets of standards that place most varieties in groups or categories, many of which are further subdivided into subcategories.

For example, a London shubunkin is a single-tailed, short-finned goldfish with mottled coloration that should include a degree of blue. A Bristol shubunkin is similar but has longer fins, particularly the caudal fin, which has rounded lobes. The American shubunkin (which is very similar to the Japanese shubunkin from which it was developed) has a particularly long caudal fin with pointed lobes. A comet has an even longer caudal fin than the shubunkin. It should be pointed and be roughly as long as the body itself.

A fantail is a relatively short-finned, double-tailed variety with an oval body. A veiltail is similar to the fantail but has long, flowing fins. An oranda has long, flowing fins as well but also carries a raspberrylike growth, called a hood, on the head. A moor is another double-tailed fish, but this time there is no hood. Instead, the eyes usually protrude from the head, and the overall color is black. In modern moors, however, other colors also occur.

Pearlscales are oval-bodied, short-finned, double-tailed fish, and they have domed or convex scales that look like pearls. A pearl-scaled fish with two "bubbles" on the top of its head is known as a high-head pearlscale, or hamanishiki. Lionheads have a similarly shaped body but no pearls or dorsal fin. In addition, the head has a hood similar to that found in orandas. A ranchu is similar to a lionhead but

has a highly curved back, particularly around the caudal peduncle (the posterior end of the body that supports the caudal fin).

Celestials have body characteristics similar to lionheads but have no hood and, as their name suggests, have upward-looking eyes. The bubble-eye takes this development further and has large, fluid-filled sacs that protrude from the eye socket.

The pompon is yet another oval, usually dorsal-less, twin-tailed fish. In this variety the eyes are normal, but the nasal septa are developed into two characteristic round pompons—an overdevelopment of the tissue resulting in a ball-shaped structure that adorns the top of the snout.

Body characteristics can occur in combination with a range of colors. To help make life easier for enthusiasts and specialist breeders, the combinations are generally grouped as follows:

Metallic—these fish contain a considerable amount of the pigment guanine, which gives the body reflective (metallic) qualities.

⬇ The sarassa comet has a red, silver, and white coloration.

Matt—these fish lack reflective components; such fish are therefore nonshiny in appearance.
Nacreous—these fish have an overall "mother-of-pearl" sheen. In some ways nacreous fish exhibit a combination of the characteristics of both the earlier types.
Calico—these fish carry a blue ground color splashed with black, violet, red, brown, and yellow.

Note: Some goldfish societies use the calico classification to include both nacreous and matt fish, provided they meet the relevant color criteria.

To judge what constitutes a champion goldfish, one really needs to consult the standards laid down by the various societies. The rules are used by trained judges who regularly officiate at competitive shows, awarding points for body shape, color, finnage, condition, deportment, and in the cases of pairs and groups, for matching.

Bearing in mind the time, effort, expertise, and expense that are required to produce high-quality fish, recognition is eagerly sought from top judges at national and international shows, where hundreds of entries are invariably received by the organizing committees. These shows have been held regularly since 1862, when the first-ever show is thought to have taken place in Osaka, Japan.

Hoods and Dorsals
The large group known as hooded goldfish consists exclusively of varieties referred to as orandas, broadly identified as those fish with a hood and a dorsal fin, and otherwise split between metallic types and calico types (bearing three or more colors), and those that have a white or silvery body with a red hood (the redcap).

However, such basic classification is only adequate for those with a superficial interest in orandas; it is not enough for specialists. For example, in the majority of orandas the hood grows in three distinct areas of the head. On the topmost part is the cranial hood, while under the eyes we find the infraorbital hood,

There are Hoods...and Hoods

Some types of goldfish can be divided into subcategories or subtypes based on particular features. For example, there are some that have a type of head growth known as a hood. However, there are even different types hoods: Some varieties will boast large hoods that cover most or all of the head, while others may display what could best be described as a light roughness (rugosity). Yet irrespective of the degree of hood growth, all these fish are highly regarded in their own way.

Oriental fish enthusiasts attach great value to hoods, but they are not alone; Americans and Europeans, for example, also rate hooded fish highly. There are even specialist societies of goldfish fans who dedicate themselves exclusively to the care, breeding, and appreciation of a single variety of hooded goldfish, such as the ranchu. Even more specialized are those societies that concentrate on a single "subvariety" of hooded goldfish, such as the Yokohama ranchu.

The fact is that hooded goldfish hold a very privileged place among virtually all those who like the more elaborate forms of fancy goldfish that are regularly developed by specialist breeders. As a result, there is a wide range of goldfish varieties that exhibit hood growth of one type or other.

Basically, though, all hooded types can be categorized within one of three groups: those bearing a hood and dorsal fin; those with a hood but without a dorsal fin; and those with a hood that consists of "bubbles" (also referred to as a crown) instead of the usual rough, raspberrylike growth.

and covering the gill covers, the opercular hood.

Ideally, all three hoods should be equally developed, resulting in a raspberrylike, rough growth that covers practically the whole of the head. Such a condition is, however, very difficult to achieve to perfection. In most cases the largest component is the cranial one. The most distinctive form of this type of development is the one that characterizes the redcap—a variety of oranda that has a white body and a red hood.

When hood growth is more elaborate and extends all the way to the nostrils (nares), it either restricts or prevents the development of another characteristic that lighter-hooded orandas and lionheads can exhibit, the so-called pompon. The presence of the pompon is normally signaled in the name of the particular variety of fish, as in the chocolate pompon oranda or the orange pompon.

Bubbles and Dorsals

There is one particular type of hood development that has resulted not in extreme roughness, as in orandas, but in a hood that appears to consist of two bubbles, elongated from front to back, each one occupying one half of the top part of the skull. This type of hood, or crown, is found in just one variety of goldfish, which also bears pearl-like scales—the hamanishiki, a variety created in Japan. Outside Japan the hamanishiki is often referred to as the high-head pearlscale.

In the past hamanishiki were nearly always light-colored fish, usually adorned in shades of orange and white. In recent years, though, other, stronger colors have begun to appear, making some of these fish even more impressive and spectacular.

Hoods without Dorsals

Lionheads are similar to orandas but lack the characteristic dorsal fin, although the spines that normally constitute the base of the dorsal fin are still found under the skin. In poor specimens the spines actually cause bumps or irregularities along the dorsal profile. To be of high quality, a lionhead must have a completely smooth dorsal profile without the slightest sign of its oranda ancestry.

Just as it is not enough to classify a hooded fish with a dorsal fin as an oranda, neither is it sufficient to classify a hooded, dorsal-less one as a lionhead. For a start, it is necessary to distinguish a Chinese lionhead from a Japanese one.

In the Chinese type the dorsal profile forms almost a straight, horizontal line extending from behind the head to the base (origin) of the caudal fin, or caudal peduncle.

This is the fish that many years ago became established in several countries and is, in strict terms, the true lionhead. The lionheads that were developed in Japan have a distinctively curved dorsal profile that results in the double caudal fin pointing not backward but at a downward angle. These Japanese lionheads are known as ranchu.

As in the orandas, the most important characteristics of both ranchu and lionheads is the hood, which has the same three components: cranial, infraorbital, and opercular. Taken in conjunction with other body characteristics, the relationship between the three hood components largely determines the quality of the fish.

However, even here there are varietal and subvarietal differences. For instance, in the Yokohama ranchu the three components should be more or less comparable. Therefore these ranchu have a good "cap" on top of the head, gill covers that are well covered in rough tissue, and an infraorbital component that gives them a full-cheeked appearance.

Yet despite the importance of the hood, there are some magnificent oriental ranchu that have very small hoods. One thing is certain: Among the hooded goldfish there is so much variety and so much still remains to be discovered that it would take more than a lifetime's work to learn all the secrets of these marvellous fish.

⊙ The black ranchu displays a hood, curved back without a dorsal fin, and a matt black coloration.

Grass Carp
Ctenopharyngodon idellus

The grass carp is a large fish that eats vast quantities of aquatic plants and therefore provides a chemical-free method of weed control.

Common name Grass carp (white Amur, Chinese grass carp)

Scientific name *Ctenopharyngodon idellus*

Family Cyprinidae

Subfamily Cyprininae

Order Cypriniformes

Size Up to 4.9 ft (1.5 m) in length but often smaller

Key features Elongated body with relatively small head; short snout with subterminal mouth; no barbels; all fins well formed with broad caudal fin; body fully scaled; coloration: generally drab with lighter belly

Breeding Peak of the spawning season occurs in April–May in China; elsewhere there may be some variation; spawning occurs over gravel riverbeds in fast-flowing water; eggs scattered and abandoned; optimum water temperature 81–84° F (27–29° C)

Diet Almost exclusively aquatic plants and small invertebrates

Habitat Large, still or slow-flowing bodies of water; abundant vegetation is important; low oxygen levels and some salt in water tolerated

Distribution Originally from China and the Amur basin in eastern Siberia; now introduced into around 90 countries from Argentina to New Zealand

THE GRASS CARP, WHITE AMUR, or Chinese grass carp is native to lowland rivers in China and the Amur basin in eastern Siberia. However, its justified reputation as a plant eater and its excellent flavor when eaten have resulted in numerous introductions into areas far outside its home range.

The first introductions are thought to have been carried out before the 18th century, when stocks were taken to Taiwan from mainland China. Since then numerous introductions have been documented, the first beginning in 1800 and ending in 1899, during which the grass carp was repeatedly introduced into Malaysia. Japan received its first grass carp in 1878 and exported stocks to Indonesia in 1915. It is not known when Thailand and Singapore got their first imports, although it is known that Singapore's stocks came from China.

As the 20th century ran its course, countless introductions and reintroductions took place. In most of cases the "source" countries were neither China nor the former U.S.S.R. but a whole host of others that had themselves been previously supplied with grass carp. As a result, this species is now found in at least 90 countries outside its natural range. Nearly 30 of them are now definitely known to have established populations of the species in their rivers, while about 20 are likely to have established populations.

Control versus Impact

The effects of the introductions on native species are complex and in many cases not fully understood. For example, the clearing of choked-up channels and rivers for boat traffic may adversely affect some local species by removing vegetation they feed on, use for

⊕ *Grass carp have been introduced into various river systems around the world to control green vegetation, but the ecological effects of the introductions are sometimes difficult to determine.*

spawning purposes, or as shelter from predators. At the same time, it may help others, for example, sunfish (family Centrarchidae), to breed more successfully.

The introductions could affect native plants as well, depending on how heavily stocked the chosen body of water is allowed to become. Where it is heavily stocked with grass carp, they may eat not just the "target" vegetation but also other plants as well. If "nontarget" plants are eaten excessively, this may even cause the "target" varieties to increase.

Deciding on the correct levels of grass carp introductions is a complex task. Where the balance has been correctly figured out, no harmful effects have been reported. However, Hungary, Vietnam, New Zealand, Belgium, Sweden, Switzerland, South Africa, and Algeria all report negative ecological impacts.

Some of the negative effects can be indirect, such as loss of spawning areas. In the U.S., for example, the introduction of the grass carp brought with it a parasitic worm. A small native species, the red shiner (*Cyprinella lutrensis*), adapted quickly to the new parasite, and since the red shiner is used widely in the U.S. as a bait fish, the parasitic worm has been introduced into numerous waters throughout the country. One place where it is having a particularly serious effect is in Utah, where the woundfin (*Plagopterus argentissimus*) is becoming rare, to the extent that the World Conservation Union now lists it as Vulnerable.

Popular Albinos

Around the 1980s an albino form of the grass carp started appearing in pond and aquarium shops in Europe. These attractive fish caused great interest among fishkeepers, particularly those with large koi pools, and the grass carp became very popular in a remarkably short period of time. However, owing to their ability to become established in rivers and other bodies of water, imports of the species (both wild type and albino) are now either controlled or banned altogether in many countries.

Flying fox (*Epalzeorhynchos kalopterus*)

Common name Freshwater sharks

Scientific names *Balantiocheilos, Epalzeorhynchos, Labeo, Luciosoma*

Family   Cyprinidae

Subfamilies Cyprininae, Rasborinae

Order   Cypriniformes

Number of species 116 in 4 genera

Size   From 4.8 in (12 cm) to 6 ft (1.8 m)

Key features Considerable variation in body shape: Apollo sharks (*Luciosoma* spp.) elongated with straight backs, upturned mouths, long, fine mouth barbels, dorsal fins set well back on body; silver shark (*Balantiocheilos*) also elongated but has large eyes, large, silvery scales, mouth just under tip of snout, no barbels, groove on back edge of lower lip, and well-formed fins that are yellowish-gold with black edges; in red-tailed black shark, black shark, and relatives (*Labeo* and *Epalzeorhynchos* spp.); suckerlike mouth located under tip of snout, barbels thicker than Apollo sharks, back of body generally curved, while belly is flatter and all fins well formed

Breeding Eggs scattered among vegetation or over bottom and abandoned; may be prespawning migrations in some species

Diet Ranges from free-floating and encrusting algae, plants, and small invertebrates to terrestial insects and fish in Apollo sharks

Habitat Mostly found in flowing waters—fast-flowing in the case of some Apollo sharks, e.g., *Labeo spilopleura*, and considerably gentler waters in most others; bottom may be fine-grained, as for some *Labeo* species, or rocky, as for some *Luciosoma* species

Distribution Mostly Southeast Asia but also found in India and Africa (some *Labeo* species)

Status Only a few species are known to be under threat in the wild, most notably the silver shark, which is officially listed by the World Conservation Union as Endangered

🔼 *The flying fox (Epalzeorhynchos kalopterus), native to Southeast Asia as well as India and Africa, can grow to almost 6 ft (1.8 m).*

Freshwater Sharks

Balantiocheilos, Epalzeorhynchos, Labeo, Luciosoma

Despite their common name and somewhat sharklike appearance, freshwater sharks of the family Cyprinidae are completely unrelated to true sharks.

UNDOUBTEDLY THE LABEL "SHARK" ORIGINALLY made these fish appealing to a section of the general public, as well as to the aquarium-keeping fraternity around the world. There is no doubt that the term "shark" continues to have considerable selling power even today, despite the fact that aquarists know the cyprinid fish swimming around in their freshwater aquariums are in no way related to their larger, marine predatory namesakes.

Another factor contributing to the popularity of these "sharks" is the relative ease with which they can be kept in captivity. For example, most species do not have exacting dietary or water chemistry requirements, and therefore, assuming that appropriately roomy accommodation can be provided, it is perfectly feasible to keep such fish in peak condition until they die of old age.

Modern-day aquarium technology and husbandry techniques mean that even fully mature specimens of many of the larger species can now be adequately provided for, especially since the demand for large "companion" fish continues to expand. The interest in the species, together with the large numbers of specimens collected, has resulted in a considerable fund of knowledge about their biology and lifestyles.

Four "Shark" Genera

The label "shark," when used in connection with cyprinids, is generally applied to members of just four genera: *Balantiocheilos, Epalzeorhynchos, Labeo,* and *Luciosoma.* Interestingly, at least one *Epalzeorhynchos* species—(*E. kalopterus*)—is not known as a shark at all but as the flying fox.

🔽 *The dramatic appearance of the ruby shark (Epalzeorhynchos frenatus), found in Thailand, is matched by often aggressive behavior, though the threat is reduced due to the absence of biting teeth.*

As if to emphasize the looseness with which common names are used, the four genera, while all belonging to the family Cyprinidae, are split between two subfamilies. The first three genera belong in the Cyprininae (although in different subgroups), while *Luciosoma* belongs in the Rasborinae, the same subfamily that contains the danios and rasboras.

Spectacular Redtail and Relatives

One of the most impressive of all these sharks is, undoubtedly, the most appropriately named red-tailed black shark (*Epalzeorhynchos bicolor*). With its velvety black body and fins, except for the tail, which is brilliant red, this species is truly magnificent. It is also, perhaps, one of the more demanding species in terms of water quality. When it is not right, the black fades to gray, and the brilliant red caudal fin becomes pale.

As specimens become older, they become progressively more aggressive toward members of their own species, which they will not tolerate in their territory. However, since this species, being a cyprinid, lacks biting teeth, no

⊙ *The red-spotted, or purple, shark (Labeo congoro) is an African species from fast-flowing waters; it can grow to around 16.5 inches (42 cm) and a weight of 9.5 pounds (4.3 kg).*

serious damage is inflicted during what are generally sham attacks consisting of raised fins and body posturing. The red-tailed black shark originates in Thailand and grows to just 4.8 inches (12 cm).

Its closest relative, the ruby, rainbow, or red-finned shark (*E. frenatus*)—also from Thailand—is a little larger at 6 inches (15 cm), as well as slightly slimmer, and all the fins, not just the tail, are red. The body is a grayish-brown all over, with a darker band extending

Dwindling Silver Shark Populations

At one time the silver shark was hugely abundant throughout its range in Southeast Asia. As demand from aquarists continued and local populations became overfished, however, the search moved into new, unexploited areas, including spawning grounds. This added to the already considerable pressure on the species, as harvests now included not just adults but also juveniles that would normally have replenished a percentage of the adult population that had been captured.

Further pressures came from deforestation, with all the habitat changes it causes, deterioration in water quality, and silting, so that eventually the silver shark became not just very scarce in parts of its range in Kalimantan and Sumatra but virtually wiped out in others. Thailand populations, however, remained almost untouched, so the species, as a whole, was not depleted to the point where recovery becomes impossible. Today, though, the Thai populations are also believed to be declining.

In recent years the main cause of decline has no longer been collection for home aquariums, since the silver shark is now bred in large numbers in captivity. Indeed, virtually all the world demand for this still-popular species is now met from captive-bred stocks. This, allied to the modern-day ornamental aquatic industry's conservation-based harvesting policies, offers hope for the future of the species—at least in captivity.

Wild populations, however, face a more uncertain future owing to numerous factors, including continuing habitat changes, poor water quality, and the use of poisons and small-mesh nets. At least some of the problems are being addressed, but it will take some time before the effectiveness of the protective measures can be assessed. For the moment, therefore, the silver shark is listed as Endangered by the World Conservation Union.

from the snout backward and upward to the eye. In general behavior it is similar to the red-tailed black shark. An albino form of this species has been produced commercially.

A further well-known member of this genus is the flying fox, which looks more like the Siamese flying fox (*Crossocheilus siamensis*) than its closest relatives. However, the flying fox has two pairs of barbels around its mouth, while its Siamese lookalike only has one.

The largest of the popular "sharks" is the black shark, or black labeo (*Labeo chrysophekadion*), at around 31.5 inches (80 cm), although it is not the largest of all the species. The black shark is widespread in southwestern Asia, and as its name indicates, it is black all over. It tends to be a loner that is aggressive toward its own kind.

Of the more than 100 *Labeo* species very few are well known; the plain shark (*L. forskalii*) and the harlequin, or variegated, shark (*L. cyclorhynchus*) are probably the top two, after the black shark.

Like their *Epalzeorhynchos* relatives, all

Thailand, where they are considered a food fish.

Spawning follows an upriver migration to breeding grounds where large numbers of eggs are scattered either among vegetation or over the substratum and abandoned.

The silver shark is officially listed by the World Conservation Union as being Endangered (see box "Dwindling Silver Shark Populations.").

Apollo Sharks

The Apollo sharks (*Luciosoma* species) are the least sharklike of the four "shark" genera discussed here, at least in terms of body shape if not in habits. There are only five species in the genus. They are all typical surface-water fish, demonstrated by the fact that they are slim bodied and streamlined, with a straight, or almost-straight back, upward-pointing mouth, a dorsal fin set well back along the body, and a well-formed tail.

Apollos are active shoaling fish that feed mostly on flying insects that fall into the water, as well as aquatic invertebrates and small fish. Their diet is therefore quite different from that of the other freshwater sharks, which are predominantly plant eaters.

At least one species of Apollo shark, Bleeker's Apollo shark (*L. bleekeri*), is fished commercially, while another, the Apollo shark (*L. spilopleura*), is sometimes kept as an aquarium fish, along with the long-finned Apollo shark (*L. setigerum*). The Apollo sharks mainly measure between 6.7 inches (17 cm) to around 12 inches (30 cm).

these sharks—despite their varying sizes—have similar diets, consisting primarily of small plants and plant material like algae and plant debris. Most of the food is either rasped off solid surfaces (like leaves or rocks) or sucked in from sediment using the underslung suckerlike mouth that is typical of the species.

Silver Shoaler

The silver, Bala, Malaysian, tricolor shark, or tricolor sharkminnow (*Balantiocheilos melanopterus*), is very different from the red-tailed black shark and its relatives. While still maintaining the overall "shark" shape, this large-eyed species (the only member of its genus) has large, silvery scales on its body and yellowish-gold fins with black edges, except on the pectorals, which are clear.

Silver sharks can grow to around 14 inches (35 cm) in length. They are peaceful shoaling fish whose diet consists of free-floating small plants, larger anchored succulent plants, and small aquatic invertebrates. They occur in nature in Indonesia, Laos, Malaysia, and

⊕ *The elongated body of the long-finned Apollo shark (**Luciosoma setigerum**) is further emphasized by the black stripe that runs down the side of its body. Its streamlined shape makes it ideally suited for the relatively fast-flowing waters it inhabits.*

Apollo Paste

In Cambodia Bleeker's Apollo shark—the species that is most popular as a food fish—is used to make a paste known as "prahoc," a widely used ingredient in regional recipes. The fish are first descaled, then gutted, washed, and pressed between banana leaves. Coarse salt is added, and the fish are allowed to dry partially under the sun. At this point the semidry fish are pounded into a paste that is then allowed to ferment.

Gudgeon

Gobio gobio

The gudgeon is a bottom-dwelling species in the wild, but specimens kept in ponds often delight their owners by appearing on the surface at feeding time, competing for food as energetically as the other pond inhabitants.

Common name Gudgeon

Scientific name *Gobio gobio*

Family   Cyprinidae

Subfamily   Gobioninae

Order   Cypriniformes

Size   Up to 8 in (20 cm) but usually smaller

Key features Slim bodied with largish, pointed scaleless head; mouth subterminal (see Glossary); 1 pair of barbels; back slightly curved; belly flat; well-formed fins, especially the forked caudal; no adipose fin; coloration variable throughout range but basically greenish-brown on the back with spotting, fading to yellowish down sides and onto belly, which can have a purplish sheen; row of dark, roundish blotches along center line of body extending from behind gills to base of tail; fins heavily spotted

Breeding   Spawning occurs in spring and summer (April–June); several spawnings can occur in favorable locations; up to 3,000 eggs—but often as few as 800—can be laid in small batches over several days; hatching takes 6–20 days depending on temperature

Diet   Predominantly bottom-living invertebrates

Habitat   Inhabits variety of waters from fast-flowing rivers and streams with sandy or gravelly bottoms to slow-flowing lowland rivers and larger bodies of still waters, such as lakes and reservoirs

Distribution Naturally distributed throughout Europe, except Ireland, Spain, Portugal, southern Italy, Greece, and parts of Scandinavia; it has, however, been introduced into most of these locations, as well as Morocco; natural distribution extends eastward well into the former U.S.S.R.

THE SLIM-BODIED GUDGEON IS A HIGHLY adaptable fish. Specimens that have been taken from their normal habitat of cool, well-oxygenated, flowing waters and then introduced to the alien environment of a garden pond seem to make themselves "at home" in a remarkably short space of time. They become bold but tolerant of other pondmates and are even happy to feed on commercial pellets at the water surface, sometimes turning upside down to get at floating foods. Perhaps more surprisingly, this delightful little fish also breeds profusely in ponds even on a diet consisting exclusively of commercial preparations.

The gudgeon is undoubtedly a hardy, flexible species. It is the ability to adapt that has made it so widespread in its natural range, which extends throughout Europe from the British Isles to the former U.S.S.R. It is absent from the northern parts of Finland and Sweden, as well as from regions south of the Alps and Pyrenees, including Italy and Greece. It has nevertheless been introduced into several countries, including Ireland, Scotland, Spain, Portugal, and Morocco, where populations have become established in the wild.

The gudgeon is predominantly a bottom-dwelling species under natural conditions, as indicated by its slightly curved back and flat belly. It also has a subterminal mouth (see Glossary) with a pair of downward-pointing barbels. The slimline body with pointed head and powerful tail show that the fish is also well adapted for life in fast-flowing water. Nevertheless, its adaptability means that the gudgeon is also found in slow-flowing stretches, as well as lakes and other large bodies of standing water, provided the oxygen content of the water is relatively high.

Survival Strategies

The gudgeon is a short-lived fish with a life expectancy of just three years, although some individuals may live for twice as long and, exceptionally, for up to eight years. Maturity is reached after either two or three years. This means that the majority of gudgeon only experience one or two breeding seasons, although they can breed repeatedly during this time if conditions are favorable.

Bearing in mind that females normally lay between 800 and 3,000 eggs, the survival capabilities of the young are considerable. Once hatching has been completed, young gudgeon gather in large shoals, and this "safety in numbers" behavior is probably a significant factor in the species's success.

Camouflage and evasive behavior are also other major contributors. For example, in shallow, gravelly habitats the back of the body is spotted and broadly matches the color of the substratum.

In deeper water, where the fish are less accessible to airborne predators, the spotting is less evident, and the body color is deeper, especially if the bottom is a uniform color.

Adding to its protective armory, the gudgeon will, if threatened, dash at lightning-fast speed into the nearest depression in the riverbed, where it will press its body against the substratum and remain perfectly motionless until the threat disappears.

Variable Coloration

Since the gudgeon was first described in 1758, the number of subspecies has been gradually reduced and is now down to one (plus the "parent" species, *G. gobio*). It is the Lena gudgeon (*G. gobio tungussicus*) from Zhigansk on the Lena River in the former U.S.S.R.

Gobio hettitorum from Turkey is the only one in the genus listed by the World Conservation Union as Vulnerable.

⊙ The subterminal mouth, flat belly, and downward-pointing sensory barbels suit the gudgeon for living predominantly on the riverbed. Its slim body is also suited to fast-flowing waters, though the gudgeon can be found in a wide variety of other environments.

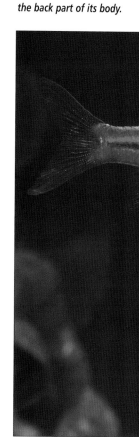

Danios, Rasboras, and Allies

Rasborinae (part)

In 1995 the zebra danio (Danio rerio) made headlines around the world when scientists managed to insert a jellyfish gene into one of the chromosomes of a zebra danio egg. The result was a new, genetically engineered fish that glowed in shades of fluorescent green under ultraviolet light.

Zebra danio (*Danio rerio*)

Common name Danios, rasboras, and allies

Family Cyprinidae

Subfamily Rasborinae (Danioninae)—part

Order Cyprinidae

Number of species Around 245 in approx. 25 genera

Size From approximately 0.4 in (1 cm) to 7 in (18 cm)

Key features Most species slim bodied; exceptions include harlequin and fire, golden, or pearly rasbora (*Rasbora vaterifloris*); danios and rasboras carry fine barbels around mouth; fins generally well formed; coloration often silvery based with superimposed patterns

Breeding Most species egg scatterers with appetite for own eggs; a few species deposit eggs on a prepared site, usually the underside of a broad leaf; no parental care is known; hatching takes from 1 to several days

Diet Predominantly small invertebrates, including flying insects

Habitat Mostly shallow waters in a wide range of habitats, from hill streams to lowland rivers; often found in smaller rivulets and streams, mostly with flowing water

Distribution Widely distributed, mainly in Southeast Asia, Indonesia, and India, with lesser distribution in Africa, China, Amur basin, Japan, and Korea; only 1 species of hill trout, *Barilius mesopotamicus*, found in southwestern Eurasia

World population Most species not under threat

Status Barred danio (*Danio pathirana*) Critically Endangered; *R. tawarensis* and *R. wilpita* Endangered; fire rasbora (*P. vaterifloris*) "Lower Risk"

⬆ *The zebra danio (Danio rerio), native to Southeast Asia, Indonesia, and India, is mostly found in shallow waters. Length to 2.4 inches (6 cm).*

GENETIC ENGINEERING HAD THEREFORE ARRIVED in the world of ornamental fish, except that the research that led to the development of the fluorescent danios had nothing to do with producing glowing fish for home aquariums. These genetically modified, or transgenic, zebra danios were produced as part of a scientific research program aimed at studying the way individual cells behave during embryo development. The adult fish, for their part, could be used as indicators of water quality because they changed color in polluted water. Since then research studies have continued and have resulted in at least two other fluorescent strains: an orange one and a pinkish-reddish one that contains a gene from a sea anemone rather than a jellyfish.

Up to that point commercial development of the zebra for home aquariums had consisted of the production of color and fin varieties, such as the long-finned golden zebra danio. However, the fluorescent breakthrough obviously opened up new possibilities for breeders who felt that fluorescent zebras would be welcomed by aquarists.

As in the case of genetically modified foods, though, such matters raise a range of objections from opponents of genetic engineering. In the case of genetically modified foods the two main sources of objections center on ethical and safety aspects: For example, how does the technology affect farmers in poor parts of the world, and what damage might we be doing to the environment?

⬇ *The harlequin rasbora (Trigonostigma heteromorpha) inhabits mountain streams in Thailand, Sumatra, and Indonesia, where it feeds on worms and crustaceans. It grows to a length of 2 inches (5 cm) and is identified by the black triangle on the back part of its body.*

In the case of transgenic zebra danios and other species, like the medaka, or ricefish (*Oryzias latipes*), which has also been engineered to incorporate a jellyfish gene, the safety arguments do not apply, since the species are not food fish. Ethical and cultural arguments remain, however. This particular debate is therefore destined to continue, and whether it will ever be resolved to everyone's satisfaction remains to be seen.

Elusive Definition

It is extremely difficult to find a simple scientific definition of what a danio or a rasbora actually is. Certainly many have brilliant colors, and all species are small, longish fish that often swim around in large shoals in nature. They also have fine barbels around the mouth and can lift their heads while feeding.

The difficulty with this type of definition is that some other fish also have these or other characteristics found in both danios and

⊕ The leopard danio (Danio "frankei") is thought to be a mutant of the zebra danio. It is found in still waters, including rice paddy fields of the western north Pacific and southern Japan, and grows to a maximum size of 2 inches (5 cm).

rasboras. At least one minnow, the White Cloud Mountain minnow (*Tanichthys albonubes*), is more similar to danios and rasboras—although it does not have barbels—than to other minnows. As a result, it is also impossible to define a minnow accurately.

Certain characteristics of some of the jaw and skull bones are also shared by danios, rasboras, and many other fish. These similarities are rated by many scientists as being significant enough to separate danios and rasboras, along with representatives of more than 20 genera, into a subfamily of cyprinids: the Rasborinae or Danioninae.

"Dhani" Fish

In Bengal, India, danios are known as "dhani"—hence the origin of the English name for these shoalers. "Dhani" means "belonging to dhan," a term used in connection with rice or grains that are traditionally grown in paddies or paddy fields. It is not, however, clear if the fish are called "dhani" because they occur in paddies or because of their small size; the former, however, appears to be the more likely explanation.

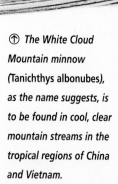

⬆ *The White Cloud Mountain minnow (Tanichthys albonubes), as the name suggests, is to be found in cool, clear mountain streams in the tropical regions of China and Vietnam.*

⊖ *The fire rasbora (Rasbora vaterifloris) is normally found in quiet, shaded forest streams of Sri Lanka. It grows to a maximum size of 1.5 inches (4 cm) and tends to feed on insects that fall into the water.*

Even then differences as well as difficulties remain because the group also includes most of the genera that do not fit into any of the other seven subfamilies that together form the family Cyprinidae. In some ways, therefore, at least some of the fish included in the Rasborinae consist of a bit of a "mixed bag" that still requires some sorting out.

Some indication of the internal differences in the subfamily can be seen in the further subdivision of the group. It is generally agreed that there is at least one subgroup that can be quite confidently distinguished from the others because of the relatively large number of skull and jaw bone features they share. All the species that are referred to as danios and rasboras, along with some nine further genera, belong to this group.

Outside this subgroup opinions are divided

not only about which genera belong to which subgroup, but even about the actual number of subgroups that can be identified.

Identity and Threats

In total there are about 25 species commonly referred to as danios. They are restricted to two genera, *Brachydanio* and *Danio*. By far the best-known species is the zebra danio, formerly known as *Brachydanio rerio* (a name under which it still frequently appears) but now recognized as *Danio rerio*.

The leopard danio (usually referred to as *B.* or *D. "frankei"*) is also well known. What is not fully accepted by some is that it may not be a valid species at all but a mutant form of the zebra danio. Crosses between the two have produced fertile hybrids—a strong indication of very close biological relationship. Further, when

the hybrids are crossed, they produce three zebras for every one leopard. This 3:1 ratio is universally recognized as indicating that the observed differences are caused by a change (mutation) in one gene. It is therefore now believed by a growing number of scientists and aquarists that the zebra and the leopard are merely two distinct varieties of *D. rerio*.

Although most danios are widely distributed and are under no threat in the wild, at least one, the barred danio (*D. pathirana*), has an extremely restricted range: the Opatha area of the Nilwala River in southwest Sri Lanka. There it is found in quite large numbers, but the mere fact that it is not known to occur anywhere else means that a single major disaster could seriously affect the survival of the species. Fortunately, this beautiful danio is now being bred in captivity.

Harlequins and Friends

There are nearly 70 fish that are commonly referred to as rasboras. Some are little known outside scientific circles. Others, though, have been popular among fishkeepers for many

years. The harlequin rasbora, for instance (now known as *Trigonostigma heteromorpha* but still widely referred to by its former name of *Rasbora heteromorpha*) was first introduced as an aquarium fish into Europe in 1906.

Like the danios, the rasboras are mainly found in shallow jungle streams or the shallower edges of lakes. Some like flowing water, where they face upcurrent and pluck any insects that fall or land on the water surface. Also like the danios, rasboras are small, shoaling fish. Most species are relatively slim-bodied and streamlined, but some, like the harlequin or the fire rasbora (*R. vaterifloris*) from Sri Lanka, can be quite stocky, indicating that such species come from quieter waters than their slimmer relatives.

Most species of rasbora, like the danios, are egg scatterers with a distinct liking for their own eggs. Only a few, like the harlequin and its closest relatives, Espe's rasbora (*Trigonostigma espei*)—also known as the slim harlequin—and the glass, or Hengel's, harlequin (*T. hengeli*), actually prepare a site (usually the underside of a leaf) onto which they stick their eggs.

⬆ *The coppernose minnow (Opsaridium christyi) is found in African streams. An omnivorous feeder, it grows to 7 inches (18 cm) in length.*

that in at least some of the species males develop nuptial tubercles during the breeding season. It is possible that these tubercles may also help during mating in fast-flowing water.

There is still much to learn about *Zacco, Barilius,* and their relatives. Undoubtedly, a great deal will be discovered by aquarists as the initial burst of popularity that began in the 1990s continues to grow.

"Different" Rasborines

There is a small group of rasboralike fish consisting of four genera that, while classified in the subfamily, are somewhat different from their relatives. Included in this so-called "barilin" group are hill trouts (*Barilius* species), which are not true trouts, pale chubs (*Zacco* species), which are not true chubs, and the genera *Opsariichthys* and *Opsaridium*.

These fish, which are often found in hill streams and other flowing waters, are among the largest rasborines: For example, the pale chub (*Zacco platypus*) grows to around 7 inches (18 cm). Many are also boldly marked, such as the impressive blue-dotted hill trout (*Barilius bakeri*), which grows to about 6 inches (15 cm).

In addition some species show distinct differences in the finnage of the sexes. Perhaps the most pronounced of them are the anal fin extensions of male pale chub, which may be a modification that allows such fish to mate successfully in the fast-flowing waters of their hill-stream homes.

Zacco and its relatives are also different from the other members of the subfamily in

White Clouds...and White Clouds

The White Cloud Mountains around Canton in China are home to a tiny, hardy, beautiful shoaling minnow. Quite appropriately named the White Cloud Mountain minnow (*Tanichthys albonubes*), this lively fish soon became a strong favorite with aquarists the world over following its initial importation into Germany in 1938. Some time later reports started appearing of a second White Cloud from around Hong Kong. This newer find had red edges on the dorsal and anal fins, while the Cantonese white clouds had white edges. Were they two separate species, two subspecies of a single species, or simply color varieties?

Eventually most people agreed that the two white clouds were different color forms of *Tanichthys albonubes,* and that the red-finned Hong Kong type was the result of populations that had become established in the wild after some aquarium specimens escaped or were released. However, the species is also officially recorded as being native to Hong Kong, so some doubt remains at least about this aspect of the White Cloud's natural range.

Interestingly, the list of common names for *Tanichthys albonubes* does not include one for the White Cloud Mountains area of Canton where the fish was originally discovered. However, in Hong Kong the species has no fewer than three Cantonese common names: *bak wan gam si*, *bak wan san ue*, and *hung mei ue*.

In English the species is primarily known as the White Cloud Mountain minnow, the official name given to it by the Food and Agriculture Organisation (FAO). However, there is a second official name, this time given to it by the American Fisheries Society (AFS): White Cloud Mountain fish. This has been adopted as the English name for the species in Hong Kong. In the Philippines it is known as the White Cloud minnow, while in the U.S. it enjoys three further names in addition to the official AFS one: Canton danio, Chinese danio, and White Cloud. In Britain the most widely used labels are White Coud Mountain minnow and white cloud.

Bitterling (*Rhodeus sericeus*)

Male

Female

Common name Bitterlings

Subfamily Acheilognathinae

Family Cyprinidae

Order Cypriniformes

Number of species About 15 in 5 genera

Size Most species 2.4–4 in (6–10 cm)

Key features Relatively deep bodied (particularly males); largish silvery scales on body; scaleless head; narrow caudal peduncle; all fins well developed, especially dorsal (in males) and forked caudal fin; coloration: most olive-green on back with silvery scales on sides of body; scales suffused with range of colors

Breeding Generally spawn April–June; eggs usually laid inside freshwater mussel

Diet Wide range of small invertebrates taken both from midwater and bottom zones

Habitat Ponds, lakes, and backwaters of lowland rivers with slow-flowing currents, usually over fine-grained substrata and in vegetated areas; may also occur in more open habitats in turbid water

Distribution Subfamily as a whole ranges from mainland Europe to eastern Asia, including Russia, China, and Japan; some species have been introduced into countries outside their natural range—*Rhodeus sericeus*, for example, now found in U.S., Canada, Britain, Italy, Croatia, and Uzbekistan, while *R. ocellatus ocellatus* has been introduced into China, Japan, Fiji, Korea, and Uzbekistan

Status 2 species of bitterling listed by the World Conservation Union as Vulnerable: deepbody bitterling (*Acheilognathus longipinnis*) from central and southern Japan and the Tokyo bitterling (*Tanakia tanago*) from the Kanto Mountains, also in Japan

 ⊕ *Bitterling (Rhodeus sericeus), native to mainland Europe and eastern Asia, have an original way of breeding, laying their eggs inside a freshwater mussel. Length to 4.3 inches (11 cm).*

Bitterlings

Acheilognathinae

Many animals hide their eggs to avoid their being eaten by predators, and bitterlings are no exception. What is unusual, however, is the place they choose to lay their eggs.

BITTERLINGS ARE SMALL CYPRINIDS THAT have unusual breeding habits. They share many skeletal characteristics with each other and together form the subfamily Acheilognathinae, which contains five genera with a total of 14 or 15 species: *Acheilognathus* (six species), *Paracheilognathus* (one species), *Acanthorhodeus* (one species), *Rhodeus* (four or five species), and *Tanakia* (two species).

Owing to their fascinating breeding behavior, bitterlings have always attracted interest both from scientists and fish hobbyists around the world. However, relatively few species have become popular as aquarium fish.

The most notable of the ones that have is the Amur bitterling, usually known as *Rhodeus sericeus*. A second species, *R. amarus*, is so similar that it is often confused with its close relative; in fact, it may be a subspecies rather than a full species. *Rhodeus sericeus* is also reported as consisting of two subspecies; *R. sericeus amarus*, found in most of the species's European/Russian range, and *R. sericeus sinensis*, found only on the Yangtze River basin.

Mussel-breeding Fish

During spawning the female bitterling develops a very long egg-laying tube (ovipositor). Males become resplendent in their courtship "dress" of shiny scales and intensified colors.

Once a male has located a suitable freshwater mussel (which he will defend against all rivals), he will display in front of any females that approach and invite them to spawn. When a suitable mate enters the spawning territory and a pair bond is formed, the two fish will hover over the mussel, often with their heads tilted down, closely examining it. The female

 ⊕ *A female bitterling (Rhodeus sericeus) inserting her ovipositor into a mussel shell prior to laying eggs.*

may, in fact, actually stimulate the mussel to open its valves (shells) with her egg-laying tube. As soon as she judges that the mussel has separated its valves sufficiently, she will insert her extended ovipositor—which can measure 2–2.4 inches (5–6 cm) in length—into the exhalant siphon of the mussel (the tube through which it breathes out) and will release a few eggs deep within the space inside the gill chamber of the mussel. The whole process happens so quickly that it is often too fast for the human eye to follow in detail.

When the female has released her eggs and withdrawn the ovipositor, the male will release sperm around the opening of the siphon or tube through which the mussel breathes in (the inhalant siphon). The mussel thus takes in the sperm, and the eggs are fertilized.

Only some 40 to 100 eggs are laid by a female, and due to the mussel's protective shell there is no need for spawns to be larger. Once spawning is completed, the male will either attract other females to his mussel or will abandon it to another male. In this way a single mussel may end up holding up to 200 eggs inside its mantle cavity.

Bitterling eggs develop in the shell for a period of 15 to 20 days. Once they hatch, the fry remain in the mussel for a further few days, until they use up their yolk sac.

Freshwater mussels also derive benefits from their association with bitterlings. Their own larvae (called glochidia) attach themselves to the bitterlings and are dispersed by the fish.

⊖ *The Rosy or Hong Kong bitterling (Rhodeus ocellatus ocellatus) is a highly adaptable and widely introduced fish which is having a negative effect on some native species.*

Red shiner (*Cyprinella lutrensis*)

Common name Shiners

Scientific names *Notemigonus, Cyprinella, Luxilus, Lythrurus, Notropis, Pteronotropis*

Family Cyprinidae

Subfamily Leuciscinae

Order Cypriniformes

Number of species 147 in 6 genera

Size Less than 3.5 in (9 cm) to around 12 in (30 cm)

Key features Body generally compressed (flattened from side to side), but to varying degrees, and elongated; well-formed, pointed, scaleless head; well-formed fins, particularly dorsal and caudal, e.g., in bluehead shiner (*Pteronotropis hubbsi*); no adipose fin

Breeding Males of many species develop intensified colors and breeding or nuptial tubercles (see Glossary), mainly in the head region; most species are egg scatterers, but many (particularly *Cyprinella* species) lay eggs in crevices and depressions; hatching takes several days

Diet Mainly small invertebrates; some plant material also taken

Habitat Most species occur in flowing waters, pools, and clear creeks with sandy or rocky bottoms; some species found in vegetated quiet areas, e.g., peppered shiner (*Notropis perpallidus*)

Distribution Widely throughout U.S. and parts of Mexico

World population Most species are relatively common or abundant, but some are under threat (see below)

Status About 30 speices are listed by the World Conservation Union in the 2000 Red List; degrees of threat vary from minor to severe

⚐ *The omnivorous red shiner (*Cyprinella lutrensis*) is found in the U.S. and Mexico. It grows to 2.75 inches (7 cm) in length.*

Shiners

Notemigonus, Cyprinella, Luxilus, Lythrurus, Notropis, Pteronotropis

Sometimes shiners exhibit localized white spots that resemble the symptoms of a parasitic disease of the same name. However, the fish could not be healthier, for the spots are breeding or nuptial tubercles, and they only develop in healthy breeding males.

BREEDING TUBERCLES ARE NOT RESTRICTED to healthy shiner males; they also occur in numerous other species in the family Cyprinidae. However, in some shiners these tubercles are particularly numerous and can cover most of the head region and sometimes other parts of the body, as happens in some *Notropis* and *Cyprinella* species. At such times the males also develop deeper colors and become even more active than normal.

Shiners are generally small cyprinids belonging to the subfamily Leuciscinae. They are therefore close relatives of the orfe, or ide (*Leuciscus idus*), the European chub (*L. cephalus*), the roaches (*Rutilus* species), the rudds (*Scardinius* species), and the fathead minnow (*Pimephales promelas*).

The exception, in terms of size at least, is the golden shiner (*Notemigonus crysoleucas*), which is found in swampy areas and heavily vegetated lakes, ponds, and backwaters of the Atlantic and gulf slope drainages of the U.S. This species normally grows to around 12 inches (30 cm) and even looks more like a rudd than a shiner. It has a keel or ridge along the belly but is silvery colored overall, thus at least in this respect living up to the "shiner" label.

The remaining 115 or so species generally referred to as shiners belong to five genera: *Cyprinella, Luxilus, Lythrurus, Notropis,* and *Pteronotropis.* Of them the largest shiner genus is *Notropis*, with about 70 species distributed in North America.

Shiners under Threat

Despite the wide distribution of shiners within the North American landmass, some species are

⊕ *The shiny body of the bluehead shiner* (Pteronotropis hubbsi) *shows how these fish got their common name.*

under considerable threat in the wild. A few of them are not usually referred to as shiners simply because they do not occur in the U.S. and therefore do not have English names. For instance, *Cyprinella bocagrande* is a Mexican species whose local name is *sardinita bocagrande*, which translates as "large-mouthed sardine." Were it to occur in the U.S., or were it to be better known outside Mexico, it would almost certainly have been named the large-mouthed shiner. This particular "shiner" is listed as Critically Endangered by the World Conservation Union.

Other "nonshiner" *Cyprinella* species in danger are *C. alvarezdelvillani* (Critically Endangered) and *C. santamariae* (Vulnerable); both these species are also Mexican. Interestingly, there are a few Mexican *Cyprinella* species known as shiners: *C. xanthicara*, the Cuatro Ciénegas shiner, which is officially listed as Endangered; *C. formosa*, the beautiful shiner (Vulnerable), and *C. proserpina*, the proserpine shiner (Vulnerable)—these two species also occur in the U.S.; and *C. panarcys*, the Conchos shiner (Endangered).

Among the *Notropis* species the situation in the wild is even more serious, with no fewer than 18 species being listed by the World Conservation Union. Among them at least four are now believed to be extinct in the wild; all

four are (or were) Mexican species, with one, the phantom shiner (*N. orca*), having also occurred in the U.S.

Like so many of its relatives, the Ouachita Mountain shiner (*Lythrurus snelsoni*) was once common and "safe," although its range was confined to the Little River system in the Ouachita Mountains of Arkansas and Oklahoma. However, it is now considered Vulnerable, since its extremely restricted distribution makes it susceptible to changes in the environment that may be brought about either naturally or through human activities.

Other species are threatened by the same factors, plus the added ones of habitat changes that have actually occurred, for example, through dam building, channeling of water courses, and so on. Others, like the *sardinita de Tempelmene* (*N. moralesi*) from Mexico, are down to just a few mature individuals in a single subpopulation. Not surprisingly, such species are regarded by the World Conservation Union as being Critically Endangered and therefore close to extinction.

Abundance...at a Price

Not all shiner species, however, are under threat. Many are actually quite abundant or

⟲ *The blacktail shiner (Cyprinella venusta) is found in sandy or rocky pools and rivers in subtropical North America and grows to a maximum size of 7 inches (19 cm).*

⟱ *The cardinal shiner (Luxilus cardinalis) inhabits temperate pools and rivers in subtropical North America and grows to a maximum size of 4 inches (11 cm).*

very abundant throughout their range. Perhaps the best known and most abundant species of all is the red shiner (*Cyprinella lutrensis*).

The natural range of the red shiner centers around the Mississippi River basin, from southern Wisconsin and eastern Indiana westward to South Dakota and Wyoming and then southward to Louisiana. Natural populations of the fish are also known from the Gulf drainages to the west of the Mississippi River to the Rio Grande in Texas, Colorado, and New Mexico.

Outside its natural distribution the red shiner has been introduced extensively in North American waters, primarily as a bait fish by anglers. Unfortunately, some of the introductions have also led to the introduction of a parasitic worm that was brought into the country with imports of the grass carp (*Ctenopharyngodon idellus*), used widely as a biological means of aquatic weed control. The red shiner has been able to adapt to this worm infection, but some of the native fish species of waters where the red shiner has been released as live bait have not.

The woundfin (*Plagopterus argentissimus*)—a 3.5 inch (9 cm) scaleless minnow-type species originally from the Gila and Virgin River systems in Utah, Nevada, and Arizona—is, perhaps, the species that has suffered most as a result of this nonnative parasitic worm. The species is now believed to be absent from the Gila River system, has become extremely rare in parts of its now restricted range, and is officially listed by the World Conservation Union as Vulnerable.

What Is a Shiner?

Cyprinella venusta is a shiner: the blacktail shiner. *Cyprinella monacha*, however, is not. It is the spotfin chub. So, what makes one species a shiner and not another? Scientifically speaking, there is no justification for calling one *Cyprinella* a shiner and not another. In fact, since the species are members of the same genus, logically either both or neither should be called a shiner. The same applies to the *Notropis* shiners in which one species, *N. harperi*, is known as the redeye chub, another species, *N. amblops*, is known as the bigeye chub, yet another, *N. lineopunctatus*, is called the lined chub, and so on.

The nine *Luxilus* species, however, are all known as shiners; so are the nine *Lythrurus* species and the three *Pteronotropis* species. In addition there is the large (in shiner terms) species the golden shiner (*Notemigonus crysoleucas*) that is only distantly related to the more "traditional" shiners.

In fact, it is tradition, more than anything else, that has resulted in some species being known as shiners and others not. Biological relationships are also involved to the extent that all the species and genera are related, but not necessarily more so than others. In particular, *Notemigonus* is more distantly related to the five traditional shiner genera than any of them are to, say, *Pimephales* (including the fathead minnow, *P. promelas*). Yet, none of the *Pimephales* species are regarded as shiners.

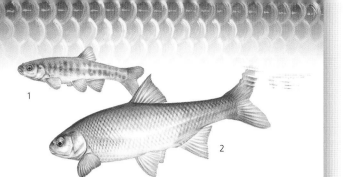

European minnow (*Phoxinus phoxinus*)–1;
dace (*Leuciscus leuciscus*)–2

Common name Minnows and dace

Scientific name *Phoxinus*, *Pimephales*, *Leuciscus* and other genera

Family   Cyprinidae

Subfamily   Leuciscinae

Order   Cypriniformes

Number of species Around 150 in approx. 25–30 genera

Size   From 2.8 in (7 cm) to 31.5 in (80 cm)

Key features Streamlined; well-formed eyes; scaleless head; no barbels; well-formed fins; no adipose fin; no true spines on fins

Breeding   Eggs usually scattered among vegetation or over rocks, gravel or sand; usually no parental care; prespawning migrations in many species, with mating taking place in shallow water

Diet   From small aquatic invertebrates and insects in smaller species to fish, frogs, and crayfish in larger ones; some plant material also eaten

Habitat   Wide range of habitats, including fast-flowing rivers with rocky bottoms and lowland slow-flowing, silt-bottomed waters; almost exclusively fresh water, except European chub (*Leuciscus cephalus*) and some roaches (*Rutilus* spp.)

Distribution North American landmass and Eurasia, with the exception of India and southeastern Asia

World population Most species abundant or relatively abundant; some under threat

Status   At least 3 species of *Phoxinus* listed as Under Threat; 7 *Leuciscus* species, including Turskyi dace (*L. turskyi*), probably Extinct

ⓐ *The European minnow (*Phoxinus phoxinus*) can grow to about 4.5 inches (11.5 cm) but is usually smaller. The dace (*Leuciscus leuciscus*) can reach nearly 12 inches (30.5 cm).*

Minnows and Dace

Leuciscinae

Many small types of fish are described as "minnows," but strictly speaking, the word should only be used to describe certain of the species in the family Cyprinidae.

ORIGINALLY IT SEEMS THAT THE word "minnow" became widely used for a number of small fish like, perhaps, the European minnow (*Phoxinus phoxinus*). These fish were probably not even related to each other; their only shared characteristic was that they were small.

Over time the term has expanded to denote small size whether in the fish world or generally. Within the fish world species belonging to several orders, families, and subfamilies are known as minnows. Although, strictly speaking, the term should be reserved for the oldest and most traditional species in the family Cyprinidae, fish are still referred to as minnows that are as diverse as the Bangkok minnow or Smith's priapium fish (*Phenacostethus smithi*, which belongs to the silversides (order Atheriniformes); the silver minnow (*Micralestes acutidens*), a characoid; the sheepshead minnow (*Cyprinodon variegatus*), in the killifish and livebearer order, the Cyprinodontiformes; and others.

Even in the family Cyprinidae the term is used for fish belonging to more than one subfamily. The White Cloud Mountain minnow (*Tanichthys albonubes*), for example, is a member of the subfamily Cyprininae. However, all the other equally traditional species of minnow are confined to the subfamily Leuciscinae. Even in this much tighter grouping there are difficulties because the terms "minnow" and "dace" are often applied to the same fish.

"True" minnows all share a number of characteristics, many of which are also typical of other members of the family. For example, they have scaleless heads, one dorsal fin, no adipose

SEE ALSO Rudd and Roach **34**:84; Topminnows and Killifish **38**:84

fin, no true spines in their fins (although in some species hardened rays can create the impression of being spines), and no lip teeth (they do have pharyngeal teeth). There are also other features, such as the lack of maxillary (upper jaw) barbels, particular modifications of various skull bones, plus a high number of individual bones in the back, that separate a large group of cyprinids from their relatives. These are the "true" minnows and their closest relatives, which together form the subfamily Leuciscinae.

Within this large group the name "minnow" is reserved for the smaller species, while the others have different names. Of course, it is not always easy to separate a "large" small species from a "small" large one. But, for example, all the members of the genus *Phoxinus* are small enough to be legitimately considered minnows, while larger

⤓ *A common dace (Leuciscus leuciscus) flanked by two European chub (L. cephalus) pointing upstream over a gravel bed waiting for food to wash down. Both species are popular with anglers.*

species like the ide, or orfe (*Leuciscus idus*), or the roach (*Rutilus rutilus*) are not.

"European" Minnow and Allies

The European, or more correctly, the Eurasian minnow has 16 relatives in the same genus. At one time it had at least eight other close relatives in the same genus, but they have now been reclassified within other genera.

As a group, these minnows are widely distributed, with some species like the Amur minnow (*P. lagowskii*) and the Chinese minnow (*P. oxycephalus*), as their names indicate, being found in the Amur River basin (which includes parts of China and Russia) as well as China itself. Others, notably the various "daces" in the genus, for example, the northern redbelly dace (*P. eos*), the exceptionally beautiful southern redbelly dace (*P. erythrogaster*), the threatened blackside dace (*P. cumberlandensis*), the finescale dace (*P. neogaeus*), the mountain

redbelly dace (*P. oreas*), and the Tennessee dace (*P. tennesseensis*), are all found in North America.

On the European landmass and associated islands, for example, Britain, the two most widely represented species are the lake, or swamp, minnow (*P. perenurus* or *pecnurus*) and the Eurasian minnow. The lake, or swamp, minnow is a more "eastern" fish than the Eurasian minnow in that it is found throughout eastern Europe and river basins that flow into the Arctic Ocean. The Eurasian minnow, which is the more widely distributed of the two species, ranges from Britain all the way through to eastern Siberia. However, it is not found in northern Scotland, most of Ireland, northern Scandinavia, southern Spain, Portugal, and parts of Italy.

All the *Phoxinus* minnows are attractive in their own ways. Males of the North American species, in particular, have brilliant red bellies, especially during the breeding season. Even some of their close relatives, like the Lahontan redside (*Richardsonius egrenius*) and the flame chub (*Hemitremia flammea*), have red on their bellies, especially the latter species, which is outstandingly striking in breeding colors.

Their Eurasian cousins are also attractively colored or patterned. Male Eurasian minnows color up brilliantly during the breeding season, developing a reddish sheen on the chest and front part of the belly, along with distinct white breeding tubercles on the snout and top of the head. The swamp minnow has reddish pectoral, pelvic, and anal fins and liberal black spotting on the body that make it look like a tiny trout. It is also one of the largest minnows, capable of attaining a maximum length of 7.5 inches (19 cm) and a weight of 3.5 ounces (100 gm).

All these minnows are egg-scattering species, some releasing their eggs among plants, others over a gravelly or rocky bottom. There is no parental care of the eggs, which can range in number from a few hundred to around 18,700 in large swamp minnow females. Eggs hatch in a few days or just over a week depending on temperature and species.

The swamp minnow is one of only three members of the genus listed by the World Conservation Union in their 2003 Red List. Its status in the wild is not known with certainty, so it is classified as Data Deficient. One of its North American relatives, the Tennessee dace, is also thought to be under some threat, and the blackside dace is officially regarded as Vulnerable, the category below Endangered.

The Power of "May"

It is amazing what one little word like "may" can do: For example, it can halt logging in a Kentucky forest and, in so doing, help save a population of a tiny fish that is officially listed

⤓ The southern red-belly dace (Phoxinus erythrogaster) is found in pools and creeks in temperate regions of North America, including the Great Lakes and the Mississippi River basin. It grows to a maximum size of 3.5 inches (9 cm).

as Vulnerable by the World Conservation Union.

The "may" in question was included in a report by a Daniel Boone National Forest Service scientist who considered that logging in the forest "may affect" the continued survival of the blackside dace. This led to an intense round of consultations, which included appeals by an environmental group, Heartwood, against the proposed logging activities. In the end the logging proposal was not allowed to proceed, which probably saved the attractive species from extinction.

In common with several other species in the genus *Phoxinus* the blackside dace contains red, black, white-silver, and dusky golden coloration. The males in particular exhibit the colors brilliantly during the breeding season, between April and June.

The first specimens of the species were collected in 1975 in the Daniel Boone National Forest (the focus of the above-mentioned logging proposal dispute). Colored like other *Phoxinus* species, little attention appears to have been paid to these specimens, even though they came from a small area—the upper part of the Cumberland River basin— whose dace populations had not been intensively studied before. In fact, it took three more years for the differences between the blackside dace and its closest relatives to be fully appreciated and for it to be afforded full species status.

Since then a great deal has been learned about this dace. Of particular interest is its

sensitivity to silt-laden water, a characteristic that restricts it to clear-water areas of streams, in particular, pools of about 40 inches (1 m) depth, fed by flowing water from narrower, shallower stretches. In general, such pools contain undercut banks and are fringed by dense vegetation such as hemlock and rhododendrons. The substratum can be sandy, gravelly, or rocky, but generally free of fine sediments. Most pools are located at altitudes of between 900 and 1,600 feet (275–490 m) above sea level.

Few fish species are found in these waters besides the blackside dace. However, one that is

⊕ *Found in turbid, poorly oxygenated temperate waters in North America and Canada, the fathead minnow (Pimephales promelas)—this is a golden specimen— appears in places avoided by many other fish.*

Smelly Contact

Like all gregarious fish, minnows keep together, sometimes in large shoals and sometimes in smaller groups, but always in the company of members of their own species. All shoaling species must find ways of keeping in contact with each other, whether by color, body patterning, or, as in the case of the Eurasian minnow, by means of smell.

Scattered over its body, this species has special cells that secrete mucus with a distinctive smell. Each member of the shoal is therefore surrounded by the shared smell that acts as a chemical bond among them. This "smelly mucus" is, in fact, so effective that members of a Eurasian minnow shoal can maintain close contact with each other even in turbid waters with little or no visibility. It also helps members of a shoal regroup if they are forced to disperse, for example, by the presence of a predator.

⊖ *The orfe (Leuciscus idus)—this is a cultivated golden form—is found in rivers and lakes in temperate Europe and Asia. It has a varied diet ranging from insects and crustaceans to small fish.*

sometimes encountered is the southern redbelly dace (*Phoxinus erythrogaster*), which also exhibits the same basic range of colors (though differently distributed). An interesting relationship exists between the two species in that dominance seems to be largely determined by water flow. Where it is relatively high, resulting in clear, sediment-free water, the blackside dace tends to outnumber its relative. However, where the flow has been reduced, for example, by direct or indirect alteration of the stream gradient or slope, the southern redbelly assumes dominance—sometimes to the extent that it totally replaces the blackside dace over a period of time.

It is not so much the southern redbelly dace itself that constitutes the main problem but the changes in ambient conditions, which can include a rise in water temperature, that swing the balance in its favor. Undoubtedly the

tched Existence

: name of the blackside dace, *Phoxinus*
ısis, indicates, it occurs in the Cumberland River
:ends between southeast Kentucky and northeast

currently known from only about 30 streams in
of the Cumberland River system. In comparison
ınder threat, the blackside dace must therefore be
ntly at risk, since all 30 streams are located within
:a.
risks is the fact that of the 30 known populations,
re restricted to stream stretches of around 1 mile
ne are actually found in extremely short stretches
ew hundred yards. Although no proof is available
re is a possibility that in the past the blackside
ırred in over 50 other streams in the Cumberland

most significant factor is the higher suspended silt content of the water in the altered habitats. As a consequence, the southern redbelly, along with other species like the bluntnose minnow (*Pimephales notatus*), not only finds a niche alongside the blackside dace but also competes with it for the available food resources.

A further threat comes from coal mines in the area. Strip mining, in particular, has resulted in heavy silting, as well as acidic runoff, and these two factors have together caused declines in the blackside dace populations of affected streams. Whether or not modern coal mining techniques are still having the same effect is not clear at the moment.

Logging, road construction, and other habitat-altering activities in the species's range are also having a negative effect on population levels. In fact, a study carried out in the mid-1980s indicated that the combined effects of all these factors meant that only 9 of the 30 known blackside dace habitats contained healthy populations of the species.

To what extent, if any, the species has recovered or declined further in these locations in recent years is not clearly known. The key to its survival in its native waters undoubtedly lies in adequate monitoring and control of the factors that change or degrade its current threatened status.

Orfe and Friends

Without a doubt the orfe, or ide, the common or European dace, and the European chub are the best-known species in the genus *Leuciscus*. Since the first two *Leuciscus* species—the orfe and the European chub—were named back in 1758, no fewer than 303 "species" have been added over the years, a few as recently as the 1990s. The newer species have no common names, indicating that they are little known outside scientific circles.

Little by little, the 303 *Leuciscus* "species" have been narrowed down to 41, some with common names and some without. Among the former are two ides: the Amur ide (*Leuciscus waleckii waleckii*) and the ide, or orfe (*L. idus*).

Chubs and Dace under Threat

With the exception of the relatively well-known Dnieper, or Black Sea, chub, whose status in the wild is uncertain and requires further study, four of the lesser-known *Leuciscus* species are officially listed as Vulnerable in the 2003 Red List: *L. illyricus*, *L. keadicus*, the Makal dace (*L. microlepis*), and *L. svallize*.

Two Croatian species are under even greater threat, *L. polylepis* being classified as Endangered and the Ukliva dace (*L. ukliva*) being rated as Critically Endangered. A third Croatian species, the Turskyi dace (*L. turskyi*), is now officially believed to be Extinct.

A variety of factors, including restricted distribution, habitat degradation, and decrease in the number of mature individuals, in other words, of breeding age, are mainly responsible for the current status of all these species.

There are also three chubs: the aphips chub (*L. aphipsi*), the Dnieper, or Black Sea chub (*L. borysthenicus*), and the European chub (*L. cephalus*), and seven daces: the Zeravshan dace (*L. lehmani*), Danilevskii's dace (*L. danilevskii*), the Syr-darya dace (*L. squaliusculus*), the Ukliva dace (*L. ukliva*), the Turskyi dace (*L. turskyi*), the Makal dace (*L. microlepis*), and the common dace (*L. leuciscus*). Only two other species bear common names: the vairone, or souffie (*L. souffia*) and the bordallo (*L. carolitertii*).

The ide is a silver-bodied, shoaling fish that prefers the upper layers of the water column. It can grow up to 40 inches (1 m) in length but is usually smaller. It is a native of the Danube River basin and most parts of Europe, but not Norway or the southernmost parts. However, it

⊖ **The creek chub (Semotilus atromaculatus) is commonly found in streams throughout large parts of the eastern U.S. and southeastern Canada. It grows to a maximum size of 12 inches (30 cm).**

large, blunt head and mouth ("cephalus" means head). Like the ide and the common dace, it prefers flowing water. However, unlike its closest relatives, the European chub can withstand a wider range of water conditions and is sometimes found feeding on waste near sewage outlets. It is a slow-growing fish that can, nevertheless, attain a considerable size. One specimen caught by an angler measured 31.5 inches (80 cm) and weighed 17.6 pounds (8 kg), but most specimens are half this size.

The chub has a varied diet, ranging from plant material to insects, crustaceans, mollusks, and frogs. It even rises to the surface on occasion to snatch insects—much to the irritation of fly fishermen who are casting their lines for trout!

has been introduced into many areas in Europe as well as elsewhere.

In addition to the silver wild type several color forms have been developed commercially, primarily for ponds. They include a golden form (universally known as the golden orfe), a marbled form, and a blue one, whose beauty can only be fully appreciated when viewed from the side. This variety is therefore particularly suitable for large aquariums.

The common dace (*L. leuciscus*) is a smaller, (12 inches/30 cm) slim-bodied close relative of the ide. It, too, is a fast-swimming, silvery surface shoaler, but only during the evening, choosing to spend much of the day in midwater or close to the bottom.

The European chub (*L. cephalus*) is a sturdy, cylindrically bodied fish with a characteristically

Golden Baitfish

A small, attractive, widely distributed North American and Canadian minnow, the fathead minnow (*Pimephales promelas*), has been traditionally popular among anglers as a live baitfish for many years. As a result, it has found its way into numerous waters across the U.S. through "bait-bucket" releases. It has also been introduced into Puerto Rico, France, Belgium, and Germany, where it has become established in the wild.

In the late 1970s or early 1980s a golden form was developed, making the species an even more attractive baitfish. This golden form also found favor among pondkeepers and aquarists, since the fish was not only beautiful to look at but also hardy, peaceful, and easy to feed and breed.

Besides being one of the very few minnows that have been produced in colors other than the wild type, the fathead is also unusual in that it does not scatter its eggs. Instead, the eggs are stuck on the roof of a cave or under any other suitable surface and are guarded by the male until they hatch.

None of the three other members of the genus, the bluntnose minnow (*P. notatus*), the slim minnow (*P. tenellus*), or the bullhead minnow (*P. vigilax*), have become as popular, probably because they have neither been used as baitfish nor developed into color forms. All are, however, very attractive species in their own right, in particular the males, which develop intensified colors and distinctive tubercles on the head and snout during the breeding season.

Common name Tench

Scientific name *Tinca tinca*

Family Cyprinidae

Subfamily Leuciscinae

Order Cypriniformes

Size May grow to a length of 33 in (84 cm) and a weight of 16.5 lb (7.5 kg); most specimens usually smaller

Key features Body robust with small scales and thick mucous covering; head relatively large; mouth terminal or just slightly below tip of snout; 1 pair of short barbels; iris of eye red; well-formed fins; no adipose fin; pelvic fins in males considerably larger than in females; coloration ranges from golden-olive to very deep (almost black) olive-green with orange underside; several ornamental color varieties have also been bred

Breeding Main breeding season in natural range extends from May to July; over 800,000 (usually fewer) sticky, greenish eggs laid among plants in shallow, warm water during 2 or 3 spawning bouts spread out over a period of around 2 weeks; hatching takes around 1 week

Diet Aquatic insects, bottom-living invertebrates such as worms, mollusks, and crustaceans; also takes in large quantities of bottom sediments from which small creatures and detritus are filtered out; considerable quantities of plant material also consumed

Habitat Mainly found in slow-flowing or still waters, especially warm lakes and pools with abundant vegetation and a soft, preferably muddy, bottom; may also occur in marshy brackish areas

Distribution Widespread over Europe and eastward to Russia and north into Arctic drainage regions; also widely distributed outside its range

Tench

Tinca tinca

It was once believed that the rich, slimy mucus that covers the body of the tench could cure human ailments such as toothache and jaundice. Also, if injured fish rubbed their wounds against the mucus, it would help them heal faster. The tench therefore became known as the "doctor fish."

THERE IS NO SCIENTIFIC EVIDENCE to support the belief that tench mucus has special healing powers, so the name "doctor fish" is hardly ever used now. However, despite the loss of its "medical" status, the tench remains a fascinating fish.

For example, it is one of the few cyprinids in which the sexes can be told apart, even outside the breeding season. Although the differences are particularly pronounced when females are full of eggs and males develop their "spawning rash" of tubercles, at all other times males still have much larger, broader, longer, and more rounded pelvic fins than females.

Loose Family Ties

The genus *Tinca* only contains a single species, *T. tinca*; in other words, it is monotypic. Remarkably, even though the species was first described in 1758, we are not sure how the tench fits into the overall carp and minnow classification. We know that it is related to the carps and minnows, and is therefore a member of the family Cyprinidae, but where does it fit in the family?

Biochemical studies indicate that the tench's closest relatives could be the goldfish (*Carassius auratus auratus*) and the other *Carassius* species. But other characteristics, such as the number of chromosomes the tench has and the ratio between the number of rays in the dorsal and anal fins, point away from the goldfish. They also suggest that the tench may not be so closely related to the ide (*Leuciscus idus*) and its relatives as generally thought. Nor do the studies throw any light on possible

⬇ Tench are bottom-feeding fish, probing in the mud with their sensitive barbels for small invertebrates and plant material. Most feeding takes place at night or early in the morning. Note the beautiful crimson eye.

relationships between the tench and other members of the family Cyprinidae.

A series of investigations examining the arrangement of certain skull bones suggests that the tench could be linked to the barbs. Yet some of the same features appear in species like the ide, the bleak (*Alburnus alburnus*), and their immediate relatives, none of which are very closely related to the barbs.

And so the arguments go on. As a result, scientists are still uncertain about how to classify the tench. Some classifications suggest it should be put in a subfamily of its own, the Tincinae, and others say that we should regard it as *incertae sedis*, in other words, uncertain, while many systems (including the main reference followed here: Nelson, 1994) place it in the minnows and dace subfamily, the Leuciscinae.

Well-traveled Tench

The tench is a widely distributed fish whose natural geographical range covers the whole of Europe. It is, however, only rarely found in one of its eastern locations, Lake Baikal. It has been introduced into numerous countries and regions outside its native range, with the first introductions, from Spain to Portugal, occurring before the 18th century.

Since then stocks have been introduced elsewhere not just from native countries but also from nonnative ones following earlier introductions. For instance, the U.S. did not have any tench until the last quarter of the 19th century, when the first specimens arrived from Britain and Germany. After that the U.S. served as a source for tench introduced into Canada in 1895. It is possible that the Zambian introductions of 1946 originated from the U.S.

Some of the links in the introduction chain are very interesting. For instance, Britain supplied South Africa with tench in 1896. In 1920 South Africa supplied tench to Zimbabwe. France supplied Morocco with tench stocks in 1945, and Morocco subsequently supplied the Australian island of Tasmania in 1867; where mainland Australia got its tench from is unknown.

Not all introductions have resulted in established populations. Tunisia, Zambia, Madagascar, and Jordan have all received tench, but none has become established. However, most introductions have been successful, producing thriving populations for anglers that fish for them and those who capture them as food fish. Tench are also established in Finland, Chile, Japan, India, Indonesia, Morocco, and New Zealand.

↑ *A golden tench, one of several color varieties produced especially for ornamental purposes, allowing the fish to be seen more clearly.*

For reasons that are not clear, introduced and established populations of tench do not appear to have had as much effect on native fish as some other exotic species. Although there are few reports available, those documented suggest either no effects or unknown effects; none refer to specific problems. This does not mean that there are none, of course. It may probably be more of an indication that the necessary studies have not been carried out.

Tough, Warm-water Breeder

The tench can survive extremely low temperatures and oxygen concentrations; it can also tolerate a degree of salinity and is therefore found in some brackish habitats in the eastern part of its range. During cold weather it moves into deeper waters and, during the coldest periods, will bury itself in the bottom mud, where it will remain, without feeding, until more favorable conditions return.

When conditions improve, shoals of this gregarious fish will feed on a wide range of organisms, mostly aquatic insect larvae and other bottom-living invertebrates, that they will search for among submerged plants and by sifting mouthfuls of mud and other sediments. The tench also eats considerable quantities of aquatic plants.

Multicolored Tench

The wild tench is a greenish color overall, but the intensity varies according to habitat. In shallow water that contains little vegetation the body coloration is sometimes referred to as golden-olive, and the fish's lips are yellowish to orange. In deeper, more heavily vegetated waters the body color is a darker olive-green; it can be so dark that it appears almost black. The belly is generally orange or golden.

The inbuilt capacity for variation has been exploited by breeders to produce a number of different color forms. Originally they were created for public parks and lakes where their bright colors would make the fish more attractive and easier to see. The earliest color forms were golden, reddish, or golden-orange with black spots. Toward the end of the last century other colors were added—particularly with ornamental ponds in mind—including red, reddish-orange, and a red-orange-white mottled variety.

Despite its resistance to low temperatures, the tench is a warm-water fish when it comes to breeding. It therefore tends to begin spawning later in the year than some of the other fish with which it is found, like the common carp (*Cyprinus carpio carpio*). Spawning in much of its natural range occurs from May to July among plants in shallow water. Over a period of about two weeks a large female can lay over 800,000 sticky, greenish eggs in two or three main spawnings, although it is usual for much lower numbers of eggs to be produced by smaller females.

Hatching takes six to eight days, after which the larvae remain attached to the plants among which they hatched for a few further days. Once they begin feeding, they will hunt for the tiny invertebrates that live among the plants. Growth is relatively fast in both sexes, but particularly so in females.

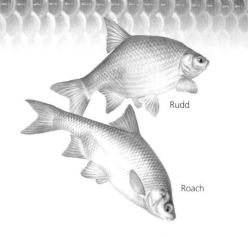

Rudd

Roach

Common name Rudd and roach

Scientific names *Scardinius erythrophthalmus* (rudd), *Rutilus rutilus* (roach)

Family Cyprinidae

Subfamily Leuciscinae

Order Cypriniformes

Size Rudd: up to 20 in (50 cm) long and a weight of around 4.4 lb (2 kg) but often smaller; roach: up to 21 in (53 cm) long and a weight of around 4 lb (1.8 kg) but usually 13.8 in (35 cm) long

Key features Rudd: relatively deep body; smallish, scaleless head; mouth slanted upward; all fins well developed; adipose fin absent; dorsal fin toward rear; iris of eye golden/orange-red; scale keel along belly; coloration: greenish-brown on back, bronze along sides, and creamy along belly; reddish fins; roach: slimmer than rudd; smallish, scaleless head; mouth terminal; all fins well developed; adipose fin absent; dorsal fin central; iris of eye red; coloration: bluish- or greenish-brown on back with silvery sides; dusky dorsal and caudal fins; pelvics and anal orange to red; reddish pectorals

Breeding Both species breed between April and June; both egg scatterers; rudd eggs take 8—15 days to hatch; roach eggs take 9—12 days; rudd females may lay up to 200,000 eggs (usually fewer); roach females produce around 15,000 eggs, maximum 100,000

Diet Both species feed on insects, small crustaceans, and plant matter

Habitat Rudd: slow-flowing or still waters; also found in lowland rivers and lakes; roach: generally similar and also faster-flowing waters

Distribution Rudd: widespread across Europe north of the Pyrennees and eastward to middle Asia; roach: widely distributed in Europe as far east as the Urals

⊕ *The rudd (Scardinius erythrophthalmus) and roach (Rutilus rutilus) require close examination to tell them apart.*

Rudd and Roach

Leuciscinae

Although they belong to different genera, the rudd and the roach are similar species both in appearance and in general lifestyle, and are therefore often confused.

THE RUDD (*SCARDINIUS ERYTHROPHTHALMUS*) IS ALSO known as the red-eye ("erythrophthalmus" means "red eye") and the pearl roach. It also has at least 34 other common names in over 20 languages. The roach (*Rutilus rutilus*) has one other English-language name: Siberian roach (used for the Mongolian populations) and around 36 non-English names in over 20 languages.

Both are predominantly European species, with the rudd more widely distributed in Asia than the roach. Although the rudd has been reported from Siberia, it is now known that the reports were the result of confusion between roach populations that occur in Siberia and the very similar-looking rudd.

From their natural ranges both species have been introduced into a number of countries where they do not normally occur. The rudd, for example, has been introduced into Ireland, Spain, Morocco, Tunisia, Madagascar, New Zealand, Canada, and the U.S. The roach has also been introduced into Ireland, Spain, Morocco, and Madagascar. In addition, it has also been introduced into Cyprus, Italy, and Australia, but not into New Zealand, Canada, or the U.S. The first introduction of the rudd (into Ireland) occurred during the earliest years of the 18th century; roach introductions began (also into Ireland) nearly 200 years later in 1889.

In most cases populations have become established in the new locations, except in Madagascar. Although it is known that some of the introductions have affected the natural balance in the rivers concerned, this has not always been the case.

Neither species is predatory, in the sense of

*Like many other freshwater fish species, roach (*Rutilus rutilus*) tend to shoal in groups containing individuals of about the same size.*

feeding on other fish, although they both feed on invertebrates. They also eat plants. In some countries into which the roach has been introduced, most notably Australia, it is regarded as a pest, not just because it churns up the bottom sediments in its search for food, but also because it competes for food with another introduced species, the trout (*Salmo* species). It also competes with some native species.

The rudd is more of a surface feeder, so it does not tend to cause water turbidity.

However, it is a species that can hybridize with other species in the family Cyprinidae. In Canada and the U.S. there are concerns that the rudd's ability to interbreed with the golden shiner (*Notemigonus crysoleucas*), which it resembles quite closely in coloration and other features (although the rudd is larger), could pose a threat to the genetic purity of the shiner.

Other Rudds
Both the rudd and the roach have become so well known that many people believe them to

Rudd and Roach Compared

Although rudd and roach are similar to each other in many respects—to the extent that they are often confused—they can be told apart on closer examination. The most distinctive features relate to body color, body shape, fin positions, positioning of the mouth, and eye color.

In the rudd the dorsal fin is set farther back along the body than the pelvic fins; in the roach these fins are in line with each other.

In terms of body color the rudd is a less silvery fish (more bronze colored) than the roach; the body is also deeper in the rudd than in the roach. The mouth slopes upward in the rudd, indicating that it is predominantly a surface and midwater feeder; in the roach the mouth is more terminal.

The color of the fins, particularly the pelvic and anal fins, is redder in the rudd than in the roach. However, despite one of its common names, the red-eye, the rudd has orange-red eyes, while the roach has genuinely red eyes.

Note: A golden variety of the rudd is very popular among ornamental pondkeepers, particularly in parts of Europe. This is a commercially produced color form that is not found in the wild.

⊕ *Two rudd (Scardinius erythrophthalmus) courting. Rudd are typically surface-dwelling fish of the reed-fringed margins of still waters.*

the only representatives of their respective genera. However, this is not the case.

There are, in fact, four rudds (though not all of them are known as rudds). By far the most widespread species of rudd is *Scardinius erythrophthalmus*. It is so widely distributed that since its first scientific description in 1758 it has been redescribed under 14 different names (other than *S. erythrophthalmus*). One Romanian population, in particular, was considered so different that it was long believed to be either a distinct subspecies or a new species (*S. e. racovitzai* or *S. racovitzae*). Its main difference is that it is found in waters whose temperature ranges from 82 to 93° F (28 to 34° C); in fact, these rudds are said to die if the temperature drops below 68° F (20° C). However, the fish is now regarded as no more than a localized variety of the rudd.

Scardinius graecus is, quite appropriately,

found in Greece. It is a slimmer species than the rudd and has larger scales. Like the rudd, it is fished commercially, but quite unlike the rudd, it is officially listed by the World Conservation Union as being Vulnerable. The main threats to its long-term survival are pollution, draining of water for agricultural and other purposes, and destruction of its habitat.

Scardinius scardafa occurs in several lakes in Italy, Albania, and Dalmatia. Few details relating to this species are available. It is not, however, believed to be under threat in the wild. The same goes for *S. acarnanicus,* which occurs in the Acheleoos basin in Greece.

Other Roaches

In addition to the roach there are 12 other, less well-known species. Most, in fact, do not have common names.

One that does have a common name is the Danube roach (*R. pigus*). Two populations of this species are known, one from northern Italy and the other from the Danube River basin. It is a slimmer species than the roach and is notable because of the spawning "rash" of breeding

⊕ **Scardinius erythrophthalmus** *is the most common rudd, found widely in Europe, Russia, and Central Asia in ponds, lakes, and slow streams. It grows to about 10 inches (25 cm).*

tubercles that males develop not just on their head but also on the back and sides of the body, as well as the fins.

The Kutum, or Black Sea, roach (*R. frisii*) is one of the largest of the roaches, attaining a length of around 27.5 in (70 cm) and a weight of some 11 pounds (5 kg). It is also exceptional in that large specimens may feed on small fish. Some populations are known from brackish water habitats, and—unlike their totally freshwater counterparts—they migrate twice a year for spawning. The "fall" populations spend the winter in the lower reaches of rivers, migrating upstream and spawning in early spring. The spring populations only enter the lower reaches of these rivers once the ice begins to melt, thus allowing them to move upriver to their spring spawning grounds.

A few roach species are under threat in the wild. Some, like *R. arcasii* and *R. alburnoides* from Spain and Portugal, are affected by pollution but are not yet considered to be under immediate threat of extinction. However, *R. meidingerii,* which occurs in alpine lakes and the upper reaches of the Danube River in Austria, Germany, and Slovakia, and was once thought to be a subspecies of the Black Sea roach, is now officially listed as Endangered by the World Conservation Union.

Rudd/Roach Hybrids

Although the rudd and the roach belong to separate genera, *Scardinius* and *Rutilus*, respectively, they are nevertheless sufficiently close to each other in biological terms for them to interbreed in the wild. The resulting hybrids tend to have eyes that are similar to the rudd's in color and fins that are redder than those found in the roach.

The rudd is also known to be able to hybridize with the bream (*Abramis brama*), the white bream (*Blicca bjoerkna*), and the bleak, or alburn (*Alburnus alburnus*). The roach can interbreed (in addition to the rudd) with at least the bream. In most cases hybrids are infertile and are produced when mixed species spawnings occur in the wild. In captivity, of course, different rules apply, since the whole reproductive process can be controlled. In the early 1990s rudd were crossed with golden shiners (*Nometigonus crysoleucas*) in the U.S. The resulting hybrids did not, themselves, breed, leading to the belief that they were probably infertile.

Loaches and Suckers

Superfamily Cobitoidea

Scuttling along the bottom, burrowing into sediments, or squeezing through the tiniest cracks, the small, slender, and whiskered eel-like kuhli loach (*Pangio kuhli*) looks and behaves like a typical loach. Lumbering along with its large, sailfinlike dorsal fin extended, its high-backed body boldly marked in chocolate-brown and cream, and measuring nearly 40 inches (1 m) in length, the Chinese sailfin sucker (*Myxocyprinus asiaticus*) looks nothing like a loach, yet the two fish are quite closely related.

From Barbels to Sailfins

Even within a group such as the loaches themselves there are distinct variations in appearance. Most people who are familiar with loaches usually think of a long, slim, eel-like fish with barbels around its mouth. Many loaches do, indeed, fit this description perfectly, although others do not. And in some of the other groups that make up the superfamily Cobitoidea there are also great variations among the members.

Yet despite the very distinct differences that exist, the suckers are sufficiently similar to the algae eaters, the true loaches, and the river loaches for them all to belong to the single superfamily Cobitoidea. For instance, they all lack true jaw teeth like their close relatives the cyprinids (family Cyprinidae). Other features include the lack of an adipose fin, and most species have a scaleless head. When certain features of the skeleton are also considered, the conclusion arrived at by most experts is that each of the four major groups represents a family, and that the four families, taken together, constitute a superfamily. This is the classification adopted for loaches and suckers here.

The Algae Eaters

Many fish include algae as part of their diet. A few species, like the silver carp (*Hypophthalmichthys molitrix*), feed on free-floating algae. Most algae-eating fish, though, feed on threadlike or encrusting algae. Such algae eaters include the Siamese flying fox (*Crossocheilus siamensis*), for example. The Chinese algae eater (*Gyrinocheilus aymonieri*) is such a committed consumer of these aquatic plants that the food it predominantly

Superfamily Cobitoidea: around 85 genera, around 652 species, 4 families

Family Gyrinocheilidae—algae eaters; 4 species in 1 genus from Southeast Asia; species include Chinese algae eater (*Gyrinocheilus aymonieri*)

Family Catostomidae—suckers; about 68 species and 13 genera from China, northeastern Siberia, and North America; species include North American suckers (*Catostomus* species), buffaloes (*Ictiobus* species), redhorse suckers (*Moxostoma* species), Chinese sailfin sucker (*Myxocyprinus asiaticus*)

Family Cobitidae—loaches; about 110 species in 18 genera from Eurasia and Morocco; species include loaches (*Botia* species), weather loaches (*Misgurnus* species), kuhli loaches (*Pangio* species)

Family Balitoridae—river Loaches; nearly 470 species in approx. 53 genera from Eurasia; species include stone loach (*Noemacheilus barbatulus*)

eats forms part of its common name. Along with three close relatives that feed virtually exclusively on encrusting algae, it forms a small group of species that are so different from their closest allies that they have a family, the Gyrinocheilidae, all to themselves.

The Gyrinocheilidae are restricted to hillstreams in Asia. They do not have gill cover spines or mouth barbels, and they have a suckerlike mouth (they are also known as sucking loaches) and a unique gill chamber design that separates them from all other cobitoids.

The Suckers

Like the algae eaters, the suckers—as their name implies—have suckerlike mouths with fleshy lips bearing wrinkles or papillae (tiny conical tubercles). However, the sucker is not used for holding onto rocks in torrentlike habitats similar to the ones occupied by the algae eaters. Instead, it is used to "vacuum" up sediments containing the invertebrates on which most species feed. This family (the Catostomidae) contains the Chinese sailfin sucker, along with the North American buffaloes, carp suckers, and "true" suckers. There are three subfamilies, with a total of around 68 species.

The "True" Loaches

The fish in this family, the Cobitidae, best fit the popular image of what a loach should be like. The body is usually long and slim, and in many species it is eel-like. The mouth is located under the tip of the snout and is adorned with between three and six pairs of barbels. These loaches also have a spine under the eye that can be raised. Most of the 110 or so species are Asian, but a few, like the spined loach (*Cobitis taenia*), extend into Europe, while others, like the Italian loach (*Cobitis larvata*), are exclusively European. Two subfamilies are recognized, one containing the more eel-like species and the other the shorter-bodied types.

The River Loaches

The family Balitoridae (sometimes classified as the Homalopteridae) are found in flowing waters, although not usually in such fast-flowing waters as those favored by the algae eaters. River loaches are slim-bodied fish with at least three pairs of barbels around the mouth. Many species burrow in soft bottom sediments, and many, like Myer's hill-stream loach (*Pseudogastromyzon myersi*) and the stone, or common, loach (*Noemacheilus barbatulus*), are most active at dusk and during the night. Two subfamilies are recognized, with a total of around 53 genera and over 470 species, depending on which classification is followed.

⊕ *The spined loach (*Cobitis taenia*) is found in both Europe and Asia. Hiding under sand or rocks during the day, it emerges to feed at night.*

Common name Chinese algae eater (sucking loach, Indian algae eater, algae eater)

Scientific name *Gyrinocheilus aymonieri*

Family Gyrinocheilidae

Order Cypriniformes

Size Up to 12 in (30 cm) reported but usually smaller

Key features Elongated body; head with sloping forehead and underslung suckerlike mouth; barbels absent; gill opening divided into two: an upper, small inhalant opening and a lower, exhalant opening

Breeding No details available

Diet Predominantly consists of encrusting algae, but also includes insect larvae and zooplankton

Habitat Fast-flowing, oxygenated mountain streams with rock- or pebble-strewn bottoms

Distribution Mainly Thailand (from where all wild-caught specimens exported for aquariums originate); also known from Laos, Cambodia, China, and Vietnam

Chinese Algae Eater

Gyrinocheilus aymonieri

*The Chinese algae eater, or sucking loach (*Gyrinocheilus aymonieri*), is found in the fast-flowing waters of hill streams in Thailand. The conditions that exist there pose severe survival challenges not just to algae eaters but to all other forms of life that inhabit these torrents.*

CREATURES THAT LIVE IN FAST-FLOWING waters meet challenges not faced by those living in more placid aquatic habitats. Such creatures include the Chinese algae eater and the other *Gyrinocheilus* species. First, they need to find ways of preventing themselves from being swept away by the strong currents. Assuming that they manage to do this, they must then find enough food to eat, and of course, they have to obtain sufficient oxygen for breathing.

As well as daily survival, they must also breed and then find a secure place for the young to hatch safely. Sadly, however, we have no information about how the Chinese algae eater mates and makes arrangements to lay its eggs in the flowing waters of its habitat.

Staying Put and Finding Food

There are several ways of solving the problem of being swept away by fast-flowing waters. For example, natural selection might favor any creatures that have the strength and stamina to remain in position by continuously swimming against the current. However, such an activity would need to be maintained even when the animal was asleep and would use up huge amounts of energy—which is always at a premium, especially when the range of food items is limited.

A second possibility is to burrow into the bottom of the stream or river and remain there, out of the main force of the water flow. This would certainly reduce the problem of energy expenditure but would make it difficult to find,

The Chinese algae eater demonstrates its ability to attach itself to a rock in fast-flowing waters and to feed on the algae that cover it. A complex gill system handles breathing.

or even capture, adequate food supplies.

A third solution is to attach the body to the substratum—for instance, to a rock—in such a way that the hold can be secured and released at will, thus allowing the fish to swim around but then rest and preserve energy when necessary. This is exactly what the Chinese algae eater manages to do.

In order to overcome the problem of being forced off its rock by the force of the current, the point of attachment for the Chinese algae eater is located as far forward as possible, in other words, its mouth. The sloping forehead and streamlined body tend to force the fish down onto the rock, just as an airfoil helps keep a car on the road.

Fish such as algae eaters have also lost the buoyancy typical of most fish, and instead they exhibit what is known as negative buoyancy—they tend to naturally sink rather than float.

Since these effects limit the algae eater's movements, natural selection has solved the problem by enabling the fish to graze off the algae-encrusted rocks without having to release their all-important mouth hold.

Breathing Adaptations

Most fish breathe by taking in water through their mouths and then

The Four Suckers

The Chinese algae eater (*Gyrinocheilus aymonieri*) has three lesser-known relatives. The spotted algae eater (*G. pennocki*) comes from the Mekong basin in Southeast Asia, grows to around 11 inches (28 cm), and is widely sold as a food fish. The Borneo algae eater (*G. pustulosus*) is found in three river basins in Borneo and Indonesia (all much smaller than the Mekong basin), grows to around 14 inches (35.5 cm), and is not regarded as a food fish. The remaining species was long believed to be a *Gyrinocheilus* species but is now called *Semilabeo prochilus*. It occurs in the Yangtze River in China and grows to around 8.1 inches (20.6 cm). *Semilabeo prochilus* can tolerate lower water temperatures than its three relatives, all of which have strictly tropical requirements.

passing the water over the gills situated in the gill chambers, where the oxygen is extracted and used for respiration. Although fast-flowing hill streams are rich in oxygen, fish such as the Chinese algae eater must overcome the problem of getting enough water to flow over its gills when its mouth is attached to a rock. Algae eaters have special adaptations to ensure that an adequate supply of oxygen-rich water enters the gills. The gill opening is modified in a rather remarkable way: It is split into two. There is an upper slitlike portion that serves as the incoming (inhalant) aperture and communicates internally with the back part of the mouth cavity at a point immediately in front of the gills. A second (lower and posterior) portion of the gill opening then acts in the more normal

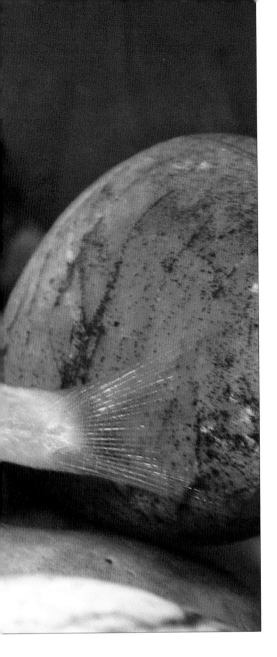

⊖ *The ornamental golden variety of the Chinese algae eater makes an attractive alternative for aquarium keepers.*

Captive-bred Algae Eaters

Although little is published about the breeding habits of this species, and despite the fact that neither courtship nor breeding has been observed in aquariums, some commercial breeders in the U.S. and the Far East have managed to get algae eaters to spawn in captivity. As a result, there are currently at least three forms of the species available to aquarists: the banded wild type, a golden morph, and a marbled one. The last two started appearing in aquarium suppliers outlets in the 1990s and will probably replace the wild type in due course.

Misplaced Popularity

Despite its generally dull coloration, the Chinese algae eater has been a popular aquarium fish ever since it was first imported from Thailand, where it is also regarded as a food fish, in 1956. Indeed, its popularity was such that for over 40 years it was considered one of the top beginners' fish. Virtually every new aquarist ended up buying an algae eater, presumably because of the reputation of the fish for eating large quantities of encrusting algae. However, several specimens are required to keep even a modest-sized aquarium free of algae; one fish on its own cannot do it despite the species' undoubted appetite for the plants.

Algae eaters are also territorial, particularly so as they become older, often sticking to and defending their patch against rivals. Target fish are mostly those of a similar body shape and pattern. However, there are other fish that can also suffer due to the aggressive attention of algae eaters, even if they look very different and cannot therefore be seen as rivals. These other victims tend to be species whose bodies are covered in a thick layer of mucus, for example, goldfish (*Carassius auratus auratus*). It seems that the mucus is very much to the algae eaters' liking, to the extent that the unsuspecting victim can be repeatedly attacked by algae eaters that graze on the nutritious mucus, often causing sizable injuries.

Algae eaters are also lightning-fast swimmers and can prove next to impossible to net in an aquarium without practically having to dismantle the decor.

Therefore, when all the adverse qualities of this species are considered, it could be concluded that its popularity among aquarists may be a little misplaced. Nevertheless, under the right conditions it is still an unusual and interesting tank occupant.

way by allowing the water current to escape once it has run over the gill filaments, released its cargo of oxygen, and picked up waste carbon dioxide.

Since algae eaters are attached to a rock as they breathe, it also follows that the mouth cannot be moved in the same way as in more typical fish to generate the respiratory water current. Again, this job is taken over by the gill flaps, which can beat at a rate of 230 times per minute. A one-way valve arrangement inside the inhalant (top) opening only allows water in, and this therefore makes it possible to create the sort of pressure/vacuum conditions that are necessary for a one-way water circulation system in which incoming water is directed over the gills and out through the gill covers.

Common name Chinese sailfin sucker (Chinese sucker, Chinese high-fin sucker, Chinese shark, sailfin sucker, topsail sucker, Asian sucker, Hilsa herring, rough fish)

Scientific name *Myxocyprinus asiaticus*

Family Catostomidae

Subfamily Cycleptinae

Order Cypriniformes

Size Up to around 39 in (1 m) but usually smaller, at around 24 in (61 cm)

Key features Juveniles with small head, downturned mouth, high back, flat belly, sail-like dorsal fin, well-formed caudal fin, compressed body (flattened from side to side), and attractive dark-light banding or mottling; as they develop into adults, sail-like character of dorsal fin becomes less pronounced, head remains relatively small in relation to body, body becomes proportionately less deep but still retains hump-backed shape, banding becomes less distinct, and fins become very dark, i.e., chocolate-brown to almost black

Breeding No details of natural spawnings available; can be bred for aquacultural purposes by injecting with hormones, and the eggs and sperm later removed by stripping (gently squeezing the eggs from the bodies of pregnant females and sperm from males)

Diet Mainly bottom-dwelling invertebrates and plant matter

Habitat Mainly found in cool, flowing rivers, often over fine-grained substrata

Distribution Centered around the Yangtze River and Huang Ho River drainage in eastern China

Chinese Sailfin Sucker

Myxocyprinus asiaticus

In the late 1980s a trade show in Singapore exhibited an impressive Chinese fish that had not been seen before outside its homeland. The only other fish that could, perhaps, share any characteristics with the new exhibit appeared to be some species of suckers—but they only occurred half a world away in the U.S. and Canada. Could these fish really be related?

THE CHINESE SAILFIN SUCKER BELONGS to the same family as the North American suckers (Catostomidae). It is the only species in its genus, and along with the blue sucker (*Cycleptus elongatus*) from the Mississippi River and some gulf coast drainages in the U.S. and Mexico it forms the subfamily Cycleptinae.

The family Catostomidae itself is almost exclusively based in the North American landmass, with only one species (besides *M. asiaticus*) found elsewhere: the longnose sucker (*Catostomus catostomus*), which extends from New York to eastern Siberia. The Chinese sailfin sucker is therefore only one of two sucker species found in Asia, its distribution being centered around the Yangtze River and Huang Ho River basins in eastern China.

During its juvenile stages the Chinese sailfin sucker has a deep body and a particularly large, sail-like dorsal fin relative to its overall body size. Juveniles also have bold body banding, making them especially attractive. As they grow into medium-sized specimens, the body retains its pronounced shoulder hump, but it becomes less deep in relation to the overall length of the body. The dorsal fin also continues to grow, but it becomes less sail-like.

Growing Challenge

Although some fish enthusiasts and scientists knew about the existence of the Chinese sailfin sucker before its first major public display in Singapore toward the end of the 1980s, few if

The pronounced fin and humped back reveal that this is a relatively young Chinese sailfin sucker; these features tend to reduce as the fish grows older.

SEE ALSO Suckers, North American **34**:96

any had ever seen living specimens in aquariums.

Now buyers from all over the world became interested in this unusual, interesting fish, and in a short time juvenile sailfin suckers began appearing in aquarium shops in Europe and the U.S. For a time they were excellent sellers, owing to their attractive appearance and ease of maintenance. Gradually, though, as people became fully aware of the large size that the species can attain and the challenge that it presents, demand slowed down.

Kept in an appropriate, well-maintained aquarium, the sailfin sucker will grow steadily and can live for many years. However, in order to attain full size, it needs the sort of space that only large public aquariums usually provide.

All the Same Fish

The Chinese sailfin sucker was originally described as a *Carpiodes* species, the best-known species in the genus being the quillback (*C. cyprinus*), the river carpsucker (*C. carpio*), and the highfin carpsucker (*C. velifer*). However, it soon became clear that despite some similarities, the Chinese sailfin sucker was different from the other suckers. Perhaps the most easily distinguishable of these differences is the number of rays in the dorsal fin: *Carpiodes* species have 23 to 30 rays, while *Myxocyprinus* has between 52 and 57; it also has more rays in the anal fin and considerably more scales along the lateral line.

Within the species itself there is quite a lot of variation, especially in banding and overall color patterning. As a result, they were originally thought to be separate subspecies. Today, however, they are believed to be no more than different forms of the same species: *M. asiaticus*.

Razorback sucker (*Xyrauchen texanus*)

Common name North American suckers

Family Catostomidae

Subfamilies Cycleptinae (part), Letiobinae, Catostominae

Order Cypriniformes

Number of species 68 in about 13 genera

Size From around 6.5 in (16.5 cm) to 40 in (1 m)

Key features Body generally long and relatively slim but highbacked in a few species; head scaleless; underslung mouth and fleshy lips wrinkled or bear papillae except in extinct harelip sucker; no lip teeth; well-formed dorsal fin with long base in buffaloes, quillback, carpsuckers, and blue sucker (*Cycleptus elongatus*); no adipose fin; well-formed tail

Breeding Spring upriver spawning migrations reported for many species; eggs usually scattered in shallow water and often over pebbles or gravel; no parental care reported

Diet Mostly small invertebrates filtered from bottom sediments and "vacuumed up" with fleshy-lipped, suckerlike mouth

Habitat Most species occur in cool running waters, often with rocky bottoms, in small or medium-sized rivers, or in clear pools; some *Catostomus* species prefer shallower mud- or soft-bottomed pools and creeks; a few occur in lakes, swamps, and ponds with muddy, silty, or sandy bottoms

Distribution Majority exclusively in U.S. and Canada; others extend into Mexico; longnose sucker (*Catostomus catostomus*) also in Siberia

World population Some species relatively abundant, but about 40% of sucker species less so

Status Nearly 30 species under varying levels of threat or causing concern; at least 2 species driven to extinction over past century or so

⬆ *The razorback sucker (*Xyrauchen texanus*), once extremely abundant in the U.S., is now in danger of extinction. Length to 36 inches (91 cm).*

North American Suckers

Catostomidae

About 40 percent of all sucker species are considered sufficiently under threat by the World Conservation Union for them to be included on its Red List of Threatened Animals (2003).

IN 1949 A FISHERMAN CAUGHT nearly 7,000 pounds (3,200 kg) of razorback suckers (*Xyrauchen texanus*) in Saguaro Lake in one fishing season. By 1966 there were no razorbacks in the lake. This dramatic decline has been mirrored elsewhere in the species's range, to the point where it is now officially regarded as being in danger of extinction. Two of its relatives, the Snake River sucker (*Chasmistes muriei*) and the harelip sucker (*Lagochila lacera*), have actually been driven to extinction. Such is the plight facing some of North America's suckers.

More Threatened Suckers

In addition, the Modoc sucker (*Catostomus microps*) from the Ash, Turner, and Willow Creeks of the Pit River system in California, the shortnose sucker (*Chasmistes brevirostris*) from Upper Klamath Lake and its tributaries in Oregon and California, and the Lost River sucker (*Deltistes luxatus*) from the Lost River system, also in Oregon and California, are all listed as Endangered. The cui-ui (*Chasmistes cujus*) used to occur in two lakes in Nevada: Pyramid and Winnemucca. However, Winnemucca Lake is now dry, leaving Pyramid Lake as the only remaining refuge for this 27-inch (68-cm) sucker.

Other species are not quite under the same level of threat, though some are officially considered to be Vulnerable, the next category down after Endangered. Yet others face lesser threats, while data on a few is partially lacking. Their full status is not known, and they

⬇ *The spotted sucker (*Minytrema melanops*) inhabits deep pools in rivers. It grows to 20 inches (51 cm) in length and is a popular game fish. The downward-facing, suckerlike mouth for which the family is named is clearly visible. The lips of living suckers are either fleshy or covered in tiny outgrowths called papillae, depending on the species.*

SEE ALSO Catfish, North American Freshwater 37:14; Snooks, Basses, Perches, and Drums 40:12

are considered as being in need of further study.

Overall, therefore, the status of North American suckers is far from favorable. Many species undoubtedly face an uncertain future unless the causes threatening their survival are tackled. Many face problems in terms of habitat changes and introduced species, while some face an additional biological risk because they can interbreed with related species.

The razorback sucker—which is not found in Texas despite its scientific name but in the Colorado River basin—has faced a wide range of challenges over many years and typifies the plight of the majestic suckers of the U.S.

The Razorback Story

The razorback sucker is one of the largest suckers found in the U.S. Owing to its size—mostly around 24 inches (61 cm) but up to 36 inches (91 cm)—and its abundance, it not only formed one of the most important parts of the Mohave Indians' diet until the early years of last century but was even used as fertilizer.

It is a long-lived species, with ages over 40 years being common, and with some individuals perhaps living closer to 50 years of age. Sexual maturity is attained between the ages of four and seven, and at an average length of

between 16 to 18 inches (40–45 cm). Upriver migrations may precede spawning, with the timing of the spawning season depending on locality. In Lake Mohave, for example, spawning takes place between November and May. In the Middle Green River, though, spawning occurs between mid-April and mid-May.

Among the most serious threats to the survival of the razorback sucker are three nonnative fish species that have been introduced in different parts of its range. Of particular note are two large North American predatory species introduced to cater to the demands of sport anglers. Both the largemouth bass (*Micropterus salmoides*) and the channel catfish (*Ictalurus punctatus*) soon exerted a damaging effect on resident razorback suckers, to the extent that large populations in lakes and reservoirs were wiped out.

In a less spectacular, but equally effective, manner introduced bait fish species like the red shiner (*Cyprinella lutrensis*), another North American native species, had a profound effect on razorbacks by preying on their young.

While these biological threats are relatively recent in terms of the razorback's existence as a species, another naturally occurring threat was detected as long ago as the 19th century and is still regarded as a

significant contributing factor to the species's decline. This time the danger comes from a nonpredatory, closely related species, the flannelmouth sucker (*Catostomus latipinnis*), with which the razorback sucker freely hybridizes in the wild. Hybridization is so frequent in parts of the razorback sucker's range that it poses a threat of extinction of the affected populations.

Away from such biological factors the main dangers facing the razorback come from habitat alteration. Dams (there are no fewer than 44 in the species's range) and the reservoirs they create constitute major barriers

Protecting the Razorback

Although the decline in the razorback sucker's abundance and its ever-diminishing distribution (it is believed to have shrunk to around 25 percent of its original size) had been known for some time, it was not until the 1980s that official moves to protect the fish began to be implemented in earnest. Indeed, prior to this time some of the activities carried out on rivers inhabited by razorbacks—such as the poisoning of part of the upper section of the Green River in 1962 to create better conditions for trout—were directly detrimental to the species.

During the 1980s some 15 million razorbacks were released in former habitats in Arizona as part of a major attempt at helping wild populations recover. Yet despite these efforts, populations failed to reestablish themselves, largely owing to the presence of the introduced predators.

In 1988 a new program aimed at protecting not just the razorback sucker but also some other native species that were under threat was implemented for the Upper Colorado River. This multifaceted project includes restoration of watercourse flows, habitat development and management, restocking, control of nonnative "sport" species, and a monitoring and research initiative. Other projects include the collection of newly hatched razorbacks from Lake Mohave for rearing in specially allocated protected areas and eventual restocking.

Just how effective these laudable efforts will prove to be in the long term will, however, be determined by all the other complex and hard-to-control factors that have brought this unique species of North American sucker to the brink of extinction.

to spawning migrations. They also remove the tributaries that have traditionally assisted razorbacks in their upriver migrations. Other water-management projects have altered environmental conditions in such a way that they have eliminated seasonal variations in water temperature and flow, and replaced them with more constant, but colder, temperatures and more even water flow throughout the year. Such conditions appear to tip the reproductive balance against the razorback and in favor of some of its competitors.

To a lesser extent pollutants, some of which are believed to affect the razorback's ability to breed, have been detected not only in parts of the fish's range but also in its tissues.

The overall effect of all these factors is that not only are adult razorbacks under direct threat, but perhaps even more worrying is the fact that recruitment—the replacement of adults that die with juveniles from subsequent generations—is running dangerously low. The future does not therefore look hopeful for wild populations of *Xyrauchen texanus*.

Sucker Splits

Three subfamilies of North American suckers are generally recognized: the Ictiobinae, containing two genera and seven species; the Cycleptinae, containing two genera and two species; and the Catostominae, containing nine genera and all the remaining species.

Java loach.

Most Popular Species

There are currently 22 species of kuhlis, but only a few are well known outside scientific circles. Some, like the kuhli, or coolie loach (*P. kuhlii*), from Indonesia and the Malay Peninsula, have been popular among aquarists for years. In fact, the species was first brought to the notice of fishkeepers in 1909 and has been popular ever since. Others, like the Borneo loach, or Shelford's prickly eye (*P. shelfordii*), followed in the early 1930s.

The kuhli loach is one of the larger species, reaching around 4.7 inches (12 cm) in length. Another is the eel loach (*P. anguillaris*), which has a more extensive range, also being found in the Mekong basin. This species is indeed one of the most eel-like of all kuhlis. Shelford's prickly eye is a medium-sized species, attaining around 3.2 inches (8 cm) in length.

The slimy, or Myer's, loach (*P. myersi*), which is also called the spiny loach—not to be confused with the spined loach (*Cobitis taenia*)—is known only from southeastern Thailand. The half-banded kuhli loach (*P. semicincta*) from the Malay Peninsula is perhaps the most popular of the kuhli loaches. In sharp contrast, the Indian kuhli (coolie) loach (*P. goaensis*) is very little known. It is known on the basis of a single specimen from Goa. Confusingly, there is a second Indian coolie (*P. oblonga*) that occurs in India but also elsewhere in Asia and is better known as the Java loach.

Disappearing Act

Owing to their slender, eel-like bodies, kuhli loaches can squeeze into holes and cracks that most other fish cannot enter. They also have a habit of burying themselves in the fine-grained bottoms of their native waters for most of the day. They then emerge in the evening and forage all night, before returning to their hiding places around dawn.

In home aquariums they tend to follow the same routines, although some are also active during the day. New aquarists who may not have heard of the kuhli loaches' qualities are often thrown into a state of despair on discovering that their brand-new acquisitions disappear completely, often within the very first day. Try as they may, they fail to find the corpses on the floor or elsewhere and often end up buying replacements.

It may take weeks or even months before they realise that their kuhlis have just been following their natural instincts and hiding from view during the daylight hours behind, under, or even inside aquarium equipment or, quite simply, underneath the aquarium sand.

⊕ *The Borneo loach (Pangio shelfordii), also known as Shelford's prickly eye, is an eel-like species from the Malay Peninsula, Sumatra, and Borneo. It can hide itself very effectively in rock cracks or under the sand.*

Clown Loach

Botia macracanthus

The clown loach is a versatile species; small specimens are collected for the aquarium trade, and larger ones are harvested for food. Despite such pressures, the clown loach is still abundant in its native waters.

THE CLOWN LOACH AND ITS sister species in the genus *Botia* belong to the "true" loaches in the family Cobitidae. However, unlike some of their closest relatives, their bodies are not long and eel-like but compressed (flattened from side to side). They also have a stouter body than, say, the kuhli loaches (*Pangio* species), the weather loaches (*Misgurnus* species), or the spined loach (*Cobitis taenia*) and its relatives.

Like all the other members of the family, *Botia* loaches have subterminal mouths; in other words, they are located beneath the tip of the snout. The snout itself is pointed and almost beaklike, and it carries two pairs of barbels known as rostral barbels (a rostrum is a beaklike structure).

Under each eye there is an erectile spine that the fish can raise when alarmed or under threat. Once raised and in position, the spines can be used as a weapon to inflict injury either to a predator or rival by the fish shaking its head from side to side.

Sideways Sleepers

When fish sleep, most species try to conceal themselves in some way. The parrotfish (family Scaridae) produce a protective mucous cocoon and go to sleep inside it; others, like some pencilfish (family Lebiasinidae), change color, making themselves difficult to spot while they are resting; yet others, like gobies (family Gobiidae), burrow into sand or seek the safety of crevices. None, however, do what the clown loach does; it takes its naps lying on its side on the bottom.

This unusual behavior was unknown until it was spotted by an aquarist who became alarmed to see one of the clown loaches lying

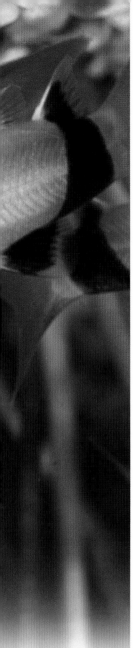

A school of clown loaches, showing the three broad black bands that break up the shape of the fish and provide effective camouflage, not least when it sleeps.

Common name Clown loach

Scientific name *Botia macracanthus*

Family	Cobitidae
Subfamily	Botiinae
Order	Cypriniformes
Size	Up to 16 in (40 cm); most specimens attain a size of around 12 in (30 cm)
Key features	Pointed, scaleless head with subterminal mouth bearing 2 pairs of rostral barbels; 1 erectile spine under each eye; body compressed; fins well formed, especially caudal fin; adipose fin absent; coloration: orange base color with 3 broad black bands, the first of which passes from top of head through eye and cheeks to "chin" area; second broader—anterior edge starting immediately behind first band and posterior just in front of dorsal fin, this band narrows as it extends downward to end behind pectoral fins; third band covers most of dorsal fin and back, narrowing and extending through anal fin
Breeding	Very little known about breeding habits; upriver migrations occur just prior to high-water season; spawning occurs in fast-flowing stretches of rivers; eggs probably hidden under rocks or scattered among crevices; no parental care occurs
Diet	Feeds predominantly on bottom-dwelling invertebrates, including (particularly) worms and crustaceans; also takes some plant matter
Habitat	Flowing rivers in Kalimantan (Borneo) and Sumatra (Indonesia); in Kalimantan species normally found in brown- or black-water rivers with few suspended sediments; in Sumatra tends to be found in turbid waters; substrate usually contains rocks, pebbles, and sandy areas
Distribution	Kalimantan and Sumatra; also introduced into Thailand and Philippines, but these introductions may not have become established

SEE ALSO Loaches, Kuhli **34**:100; Loach, Weather **34**:106; Parrotfish **40**:88

on its side, hardly breathing, and apparently dying on the bottom of the tank. However, as soon as the fish was disturbed, it simply "got up" and swam away at its usual lightning speed.

Over the years this behavior has been observed many times and is now accepted as perfectly normal not only in the clown loach but also in some of its closest relatives. It just happens to be the way these fish rest; while most other fish species sleep upright, loaches opt for a sideways-on posture.

In fact, some specimens go even further, finding a suitable spot among plants and going to sleep with their snouts pointing downward and their tails vertically upward. Sometimes they even pile up on top of each other against a rock or a log and go to sleep.

Quite why clown loaches and, at least, some other *Botia* loaches engage in this unusual behavior is not known, nor do we know if they behave this way in the wild.

Exploited but Abundant

The clown loach is a widely exploited species. Young specimens are collected for home aquariums, while larger ones—the species can reach nearly 16 inches (40 cm) in length—are sometimes regarded as food fish.

Spawning occurs after an upriver migration just before the high-water season. Soon after, the young, which occur in huge shoals, move

Other *Botias*

There are 29 species of *Botia* currently known. Some are strikingly colored, for example, the redtail botia (*B. modesta*) in which all the fins are red, and the body is a beautiful shade of blue. The appropriately named zebra loach (*B. striata*) has striped body patterning; the Pakistan loach, or Y-loach (*B. lohachata*), has almost black markings, some in the shape of a "Y," on a cream-colored base; the banded loach (*B. helodes*) is more subtly colored.

Most *Botia* loaches have achieved considerable popularity as aquarium fish, but none—with one notable exception—is under threat in the wild. The exception is the tiny chain, or dwarf, loach (*B. sidthimunki*) from northern India and northern Thailand, which is rated by the World Conservation Union as being Critically Endangered. There are, however, some signs that numbers may perhaps be recovering in the wild.

is little demand for large clown loaches; so even if their export were allowed, no overcollection of mature specimens would be likely to occur.

Therefore, through a combination of factors breeding populations of the clown loach are protected, at least from collectors.

⊖ *The 4-inch (10-cm) long Bengal loach (Botia dario) occupies clear mountain streams in India and Bangladesh. Like several other loaches, it is a popular aquarium species.*

⊖ *The redtail botia, or red-finned loach (Botia modesta), is found in large rivers with muddy substrates or in flooded fields in Asia, particularly the Mekong basin. It has striking red fins and a blue body coloration.*

down into the shallow areas of some of the larger rivers of Sumatra (in Indonesia) and Kalimantan (Borneo). It is then that most of the collecting for aquariums takes place. Yet despite high demand, the clown loach is still abundant in its native waters. The seasonal nature of the harvesting, allied to the very large numbers of young that are produced every year, are two major contributing factors.

In addition, Indonesia prohibits the export of specimens larger than 4 inches (10 cm), thus protecting future breeding populations. In any case the size preferred by aquarists is around 1.6 inches (4 cm), which is the size attained by the attractively marked juveniles as they migrate downriver from the spawning grounds.

As they grow, the bold black bands on the orangeish base body color become less sharply defined and a little faded. This feature, allied to the size of the fish, also makes large specimens less attractive for aquariums. As a result, there

Weather Loach

Misgurnus fossilis

The weather loach gets its curious name because of its ability to sense stormy weather. At the imminent onset of such conditions the fish becomes hyperactive and takes gulps of air from the water surface.

Common name Weather loach (European weather loach, pond loach, weather fish)

Scientific name *Misgurnus fossilis*

Family   Cobitidae

Subfamily Cobitinae

Order   Cypriniformes

Size   Up to a maximum of nearly 14 in (35 cm) but usually a little smaller

Key features Elongated, eel-like body; smallish head with underslung mouth; 5 pairs of barbels; smallish eyes located high on side of head; erectile spine under each eye; sightly rounded dorsal and caudal fins; small anal fin; adipose fin absent; body covered in thick slime; dull light brown coloration with several dark bands extending from behind head to base of caudal fin

Breeding Spawning from April to June among plants in shallow water; egg laying may extend over several weeks with as many as 170,000 eggs reported (although much smaller spawns are more common); hatching 8–10 days; newly hatched larvae have small, ribbonlike external gills that help them breathe in oxygen-poor waters into which they are frequently born

Diet   Bottom-living invertebrates, including worms, mollusks, and insect larvae; some plant material may also be eaten

Habitat   Mainly lowland still waters like floodplains, backwaters, ponds, and marshes—areas that may have fine-grained bottoms with low levels of oxygen, and that may dry up; usually these habitats also heavily vegetated

Distribution Widely distributed in Europe from France, Denmark, and Holland as far eastward as Caspian Sea; absent from southern areas, British Isles, and Scandinavia

ALL *MISGURNUS* SPECIES EXHIBIT THE generalized loach body characteristics, having eel-like, elongated bodies that are almost cylindrical in cross-section. They have a smallish head in relation to the body, a subterminal mouth, and five pairs of barbels. The largest of them are on the upper lip and are known as rostral barbels. Like their relatives the *Botia* loaches, all the weather loaches carry an erectile spine under their eye that they can use as a defensive weapon by shaking the head from side to side.

Of the three species mentioned here, the European weather loach is the most distinctly marked: It has several dark body bands running lengthwise from behind the head to the base of the tail. The body is also covered in a rich mucous layer that makes it feel slimy.

Burping and Whistling

Despite being more distinctly marked than some other loaches, the weather loach is still a generally drab-colored fish that spends most of the daylight hours hiding or buried in bottom sediments with just its eyes (which are located high up on the head) above the surface. (In fact, the weather loach is so at home under the substrate that if the water in its habitat temporarily dries up, the fish can bury itself into mud and aestivate—in other words, go into a period of summer dormancy. It also burrows into mud during particularly cold winter spells.)

As evening approaches, the weather loach becomes more active and sets out in search of its food, which consists mostly of bottom-living invertebrates, particularly worms, mollusks, and insect larvae. It also eats some plant material.

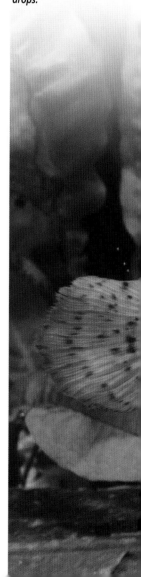

⊍ Buried in sediments during the day, the weather loach emerges at night to feed on small mollusks on the sandy river bed. Normally placid, it becomes agitated when the atmospheric pressure drops.

 SEE ALSO Loach, Clown **34**:102

Toward dawn the weather loach returns to its normal daytime activity of doing nothing or very little. However, if the atmospheric (barometric) pressure drops, as it does before a storm, the weather loach leaves its resting place and becomes hyperactive, even if the storm breaks in the middle of the day.

The reason for the unusual bouts of activity is that the drop in atmospheric pressure causes a drop in the pressure of the gas that the weather loach has inside its swim bladder. If the drop in pressure is significant, it can also lower the levels of dissolved oxygen in the water—especially in low-oxygen habitats where the weather loach is commonly found.

These conditions cause the weather loach to rise to the surface to take gulps of air, making slapping or smacking sounds as it does so. It also releases some of its stale or used air in a series of burps. More unusually, it can also "break wind," releasing the air through its anus with a whistling sound!

Oriental Relatives

The dojo, or Chinese or Japanese weather loach (*M. anguillicaudatus*), is widely distributed in northeastern Asia. Like its European relative, it is a peaceful bottom dweller with "weather-forecasting" abilities. It is usually smaller than the weather loach, growing to around 8 inches (20 cm) or slightly larger. Its body patterning is more mottled than in the European species, which has longitudinal bands running along the sides of the body.

Both the dojo and the European weather loach occur in two color forms: the wild type as well as a golden one that has been developed for aquariums.

The third species in the genus, known as the Chinese fine-scaled weather loach (*M. mizolepis*), is only known in its wild form, which is heavily mottled grayish-brown on the back fading to lighter shades along the belly. The Chinese fine-scaled weather loach is similar to the dojo in overall size.

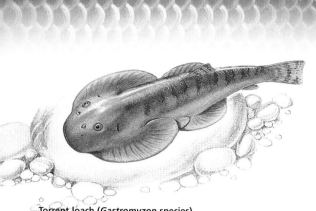

Torrent loach (*Gastromyzon* species)

Common name River or torrent loaches and allies

Family Balitoridae (Homalopteridae)

Subfamilies Noemacheilinae (Nemacheilinae), Balitorinae

Order Cypriniformes

Number of species Around 470 in around 53 genera

Size Most species around 4–6 in (10–15 cm); some around 2 in (5 cm)

Key features All species elongate to some degree—some almost eel-like, especially in Noemacheilinae; 2 general body shapes in Balitorinae: tribe Balitorini have elongated, not excessively flattened bodies; 2 or more unbranched front rays in pectoral and pelvic fins; tribe Gastromyzontini have less elongated bodies but with significantly depressed front part; 1 unbranched front ray in pectoral and pelvic fins; fins generally circular and together with fold of skin that extends between them form suckerlike structure; in Balitoridae head has underslung mouth bearing 3 or more pairs of barbels; fins generally well formed, some modified into suckers; caudal fin often with longer lower lobe in species inhabiting areas of strong currents

Breeding Breeding behavior unknown for Balitorinae; better known in some Noemacheilinae: adults usually gather at spawning grounds; up to 80,000 eggs produced in some species; eggs scattered among plants; hatching 14–16 days

Diet Mostly bottom-living invertebrates; many species from torrential streams feed primarily on encrusting algae

Habitat Most species found in flowing water whose force may range from gentle currents to torrents; bottom mostly rocky or pebbly but may be fine grained and vegetated in some instances, e.g., in some stone loach habitats

Distribution Widely distributed throughout Europe and Asia

⬆ *Torrent loaches (*Gastromyzon *species) are native to Asia, mostly Borneo, and some species reach 4 inches (10 cm) in length.*

River or Torrent Loaches and Allies

Balitoridae

The diverse members of this large family all share one common characteristic: They spend their lives on or close to the bottom, thus avoiding being swept away by the current.

AS MIGHT BE EXPECTED FROM such a large collection of species, it is difficult to find many features that all the members of the family Balitoridae share. Not surprisingly, therefore, these fish are classified differently by different scientists. Many, for example, group the stone loach (*Noemacheilus [Nemacheilus] barbatulus*) and all its relatives in the family Cobitidae, in other words, the family that contains the kuhli loaches, weather loaches, *Botia* loaches, and so on. However, the main reference followed in this set of books (Nelson, 1994) groups the stone loach and its relatives in the same family as the Hong Kong pleco (*Pseudogastromyzon myersi*) and relatives.

According to this classification, there are two subfamilies in the family Balitoridae or Homalopteridae. The first, the Noemacheilinae (Nemacheilinae), contains the stone loach and its allies—about 350 species in total. The second, the Balitorinae—also known as the flat loaches—contains torrent species like the Hong Kong pleco and relatives (about 120 species).

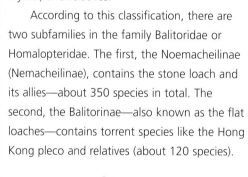

Flat...and Flatter Loaches

While the stone loach is almost certainly the best-known representative of its subfamily, its relatives in the Balitorinae, or flat loaches, are less well known outside their home ranges. A few species, however, have become popular in the U.S. and Europe mainly because they are regularly imported for home aquariums.

Among them the saddled hill-stream loach (*Homaloptera orthogoniata*) has become popular since the 1980s. It is a modest-sized loach about 4.8 inches (12 cm) in length. It is beautifully patterned, with a cream- or tan-colored head and broad chocolate-brown and tan banding along the body. There is also a thin chocolate-brown stripe running from the tip of the snout backward and upward through the eye. Another band runs from the eye down to the throat area. Like many of its relatives, it is a peaceful bottom dweller that thrives in high-oxygen habitats in mountain streams.

The saddled hill-stream loach, along with the other members of its genus, plus those of 12 others, are grouped by Nelson in the tribe Balitorini. Although well adapted to bottom living in flowing waters, these loaches are not excessively flattened.

The 2-inch (5-cm) long Hong Kong, or butterfly, pleco, also known as Myer's hill-stream loach or ornate pseudogastromyzon, is very different. Like other members of the Gastromyzontini, it has a much more flattened body. Furthermore, the pectoral and pelvic fins are circular, and when pressed against a rock, they form a sucker that prevents the fish being swept away by strong currents. The sucker effect is completed by a fold of skin extending from the pectorals to the pelvics. A suckerlike mouth also helps the fish stay attached.

Hong Kong Pleco—Not a Pleco

Although *Pseudogastromyzon myersi* and its closest relatives are often referred to as plecos, the term "pleco" is more correctly applied to several members of the suckermouth catfish family (Loricariidae), particularly those belonging to the genera *Hypostomus*, *Glyptoperichthys*, and *Liposarcus*.

⬇ *The saddled hill-stream loach (Homaloptera orthogoniata), found in mountain streams in Laos, Thailand, and Indonesia, merges easily into the background vegetation with its mottled camouflage.*

Common name Stone loach

Scientific name *Noemacheilus (Nemacheilus) barbatulus*

Family Balitoridae (Homalopteridae)

Subfamily Noemacheilinae (Nemacheilinae)

Order Cypriniformes

Size Up to 6 in (15 cm); usually about 4 in (10 cm)

Key features Elongated body; front half almost cylindrical in cross-section, becoming flattened side to side farther back; moderately sized head and eyes; eye spine absent; small, ventrally placed mouth with 3 pairs of barbels: 2 on upper lip and 1 at each corner of mouth; tiny nonoverlapping scales on body; well-formed fins, tail fin relatively large and almost straight edged; greenish-brown color along back with irregular patches, fading to lighter colors along sides of body; yellowish belly

Breeding Unusually, both sexes may develop nuptial tubercles (see Glossary) on pelvic fins (more prominent in males) during breeding season (from April to June in most areas); breeding adults may gather at spawning ponds; as many as 80,000 eggs may be laid by large females in 2–3 batches; eggs usually scattered among plants or stones; some reports indicate that eggs may be deposited in a cavity and may be guarded by female; hatching takes about 14–16 days; young may take 2–3 years to mature

Diet Mainly bottom-dwelling invertebrates; may also feed on fish eggs and some plant matter

Habitat Mainly central and upper reaches of flowing watercourses with clear waters of varying chemical composition but relatively pollution free and with generally high levels of dissolved oxygen; also found in ponds, quarries, and lakes; also occurs in vegetated waters; frequently found over rocky or pebbly substrata but may also occur over fine-grained sediments

Distribution Widely distributed from Ireland, where it was introduced, eastward through Europe all the way to China, with a few notable exceptions

Stone Loach *Noemacheilus barbatulus*

The stone loach can thrive in acidic or alkaline conditions. It can even live in brackish water. However, what it cannot tolerate is poor water quality or low oxygen levels: Its presence in a river is therefore a sign that the water is "healthy."

THE EXTREMELY WIDE RANGE OF WATER conditions that this small species can tolerate is no doubt one of the reasons why it is found from the British Isles all the way to eastern China. It was originally absent from Ireland but has been introduced there. It is still absent from the Iberian Peninsula, Greece, central and southern Italy, and the northern parts of Scotland, Sweden, and Norway.

Extra Oxygen Supplies

It is not clear if every population is equally tolerant of varying water chemistry conditions, though most, if not all, cannot tolerate polluted water or water in which the oxygen level is low. The need for oxygen is reflected in the fact that the stone loach is usually found in flowing water, often in the middle or upper reaches of watercourses where the concentration of dissolved oxygen is highest. It can also occur in ponds or larger bodies of more or less standing water, but then it is usually found close to the source of incoming water or else in the tributaries or runoffs from these habitats.

Under unfavorable environmental conditions, such as in turbid water caused by heavy rains, the stone loach can use its gut as an additional breathing organ, the rich blood supply helping it extract oxygen from the water. However, this is only a device that is brought into use to enable the fish to survive temporarily under such conditions; it is not used when oxygen levels are more normal.

Strict Bottom Hugger

The stone loach is a strict bottom dweller, preferring stretches of streams strewn with

⊕ *The stone loach inhabits areas of fast-flowing water with stony or gravel bottoms, which it mimicks with its coloring. Hiding during the day, it feeds under cover of darkness at night.*

stones or pebbles, hence its name. Nevertheless, it can also be found in heavily vegetated watercourses with muddy or fine-grained bottoms.

The daylight hours are usually spent hiding among plants or under stones. As evening approaches, the stone loach leaves its hiding place and sets off in search of food. This consists primarily of small invertebrates, including crustaceans, worms, aquatic insect larvae, and nymphs; it may also consume fish eggs and some plant material.

Its elongated cylindrical body, with which it swims in a snakelike manner, allows the stone loach to get into tiny cracks and holes from which it can extract its prey. Three pairs of downpointing mouth barbels help it feel and "taste" its prey during its night forages.

Three-pronged Attack

In the past the stone loach was gathered in substantial quantities for human consumption; its flesh is considered by some to be extremely tasty. Now, however, the practice is much restricted, although the species is still highly regarded by gourmets in certain parts of its range.

Perhaps more significant are the numbers caught for use as bait fish by anglers. Also, in areas where trout (*Salmo* species) occur, either naturally or as introduced stocks, the stone loach is heavily preyed on by the trout.

Despite this "three-pronged" attack on its numbers, plus the effects of pollution in parts of the range, the stone loach is still abundant overall, although some local populations are believed to be declining.

Glossary

Words in SMALL CAPITALS refer to other entries in the glossary.

Abbreviated heterocercal term used to describe a HETEROCERCAL TAIL in which the upper lobe is less extended than in a typical heterocercal tail

Adaptation features of an organism that adjust it to its environment; NATURAL SELECTION favors the survival of individuals whose adaptations fit them to their surroundings better than other individuals

Adipose fin fatty fin located behind rayed DORSAL FIN in some fish

Adult fully grown animal that has reached breeding age

Agonistic any activity, aggressive or submissive, related to fighting

Air bladder see SWIM BLADDER

Ammocete larva filter-feeding lamprey LARVA

Ampullae of Lorenzini jelly-filled tubes on the head of sharks and relatives; responsible for detecting weak electrical impulses

Anadromous term describing a SPECIES that spends part of its life in the sea and part in freshwater habitats

Anal fin FIN located near the anus

Appendicula outgrowths from the umbilical cord of some sharks; appendicula enhance an embryo's ability to absorb UTERINE MILK

Aquatic associated with, or living in, water

Arborescent organ treelike modifications of GILL tissues found in air-breathing species like walking catfish

Atriopore small aperture in lancelets corresponding to the atrial, or exhalant, SIPHON in sea squirts

Barbel whiskerlike, filamentous sensory growth on the jaws of some fish, including catfish

Benthic occurring, or living, on the bottom

Brackish water water that contains salt in sufficient quantities to distinguish it from fresh water but not enough to make it sea water; brackish water is found in estuaries, mangrove swamps, and other habitats where fresh water and sea water mix

Branchiostegal rays flattish, riblike bones located ventrally behind the GILL covers and making up the floor of the gill chamber

Brood offspring of a single birth or clutch of eggs

Brood pouch structure formed from FINS or plates of a parent fish in which fertilized eggs are placed to hatch safely

Bubble nest nest of bubbles that harbors eggs or offspring of some fish

Camouflage markings or features of a creature that aid concealment

Carnivore creature whose diet consists exclusively of other animals

Cartilaginous formed of cartilage

Catadromous term describing a

SPECIES that migrates from fresh water to the sea for spawning

Caudal fin "tail" FIN

Caudal peduncle part of the body where the tail begins

Caudodorsal term describing an extension of the CAUDAL FIN onto the back of the body; this fin contains RAYS but no spines; caudodorsal fins are found in catfish of the family Plotosidae

Cephalic shield head shield formed by bony plates, as found in upside-down catfish

Cephalofoil term used to describe the "'hammer" of hammerhead sharks; thought to provide lift and maneuverability

Cerebellum part of the hindbrain involved in the coordinated activity of muscles, posture, and movement

Cerebral hemispheres pair of symmetrical, rounded, convoluted tissue masses that form the largest part of the brain in many organisms, e.g., mammals

Chordata PHYLUM of animals having a single, hollow dorsal nerve cord, a NOTOCHORD, GILL SLITS, and a postanal tail; some of these characteristics may only be present in the earliest stages of development

Chromatophore pigment-containing cell whose shape or color can be altered

Chromosome tiny, rod-shaped structure in the cell NUCLEUS; chromosomes contain DNA, which carries genetic information

Cilium (*pl.* **cilia**) tiny, hairlike structure growing out from the surface of some cells; cilia are capable of whiplike actions and can facilitate movement

Cirrus (*pl.* **cirri**) hairlike or tentaclelike growth, e.g., as found on the nostrils, supraorbital area, and nose in some blennies

CITES Convention on International Trade in Endangered Species; an agreement between nations that restricts international trade to permitted levels through licensing and administrative controls; rare animals and plants are assigned categories

Claspers structures between the PELVIC FINS of male cartilaginous fish that allow them to clasp a female during mating, and that facilitate the transfer of sperm

Class taxonomic level below PHYLUM and above ORDER

Cloaca single chamber into which anal, urinary, and genital ducts (canals) open

Clone identical cell or individual derived from a single cell, e.g., an egg

Community all the animals and plants that live together in a HABITAT

Compressed term used to describe a structure that is flattened from side to side

Cone cone-shaped light-sensitive cell in the retina of the eye; cones are particularly sensitive to colors (see ROD)

Copepoda subclass of small crustaceans, some of which are parasitic; copepods do not have a hard carapace (shell) but have a single, centrally placed eye

Cosmoid scale type of SCALE found in many fossil and some primitive fish

Countershading color distribution seen in many fish in which the back is darker than the belly

Crepuscular active at twilight

Cryptic coloration camouflage-type coloration that helps organisms blend in with their surroundings; some species are cryptically colored at all times, while others, e.g., many squirrelfish, are cryptic during the day and more brightly colored at night

Ctenoid scale similar to the CYCLOID SCALE but with a toothed posterior edge rather than a smooth or wavy (crenulated) one

Cusp point or prominence, often on a tooth

Cycloid scale thin, flexible overlapping scale, roughly the shape of a human finger nail, found in modern bony fish and the primitive bowfin (*Amia calva*); the front edge of each scale is embedded in a special pouch in the surface of the skin; the back edge is free and smooth or wavy (crenulated) but not toothed as in CTENOID SCALES

Dendritic finely branched

Denticle small, toothlike scale found in sharks and some of their closest relatives (see PLACOID SCALE)

Depressed term used to describe a structure that is flattened from top to bottom

Detritus debris consisting of fragments of dead plants and animals

Dimorphism existence of two distinct forms

Dioecious having separate sexes (see HERMAPHRODITE)

Display any fairly conspicuous pattern of behavior that conveys specific information to others, usually to members of the same species; often associated with "courtship" but also in other activities, e.g., threat displays

Diurnal active during the day

DNA (deoxyribonucleic acid) the substance that makes up the main part of the chromosomes of all living things; DNA is the carrier of genetic information

Dorsal relating to the upper surface

Dorsal fin(s) FIN(s) on the back of a fish

Electrocyte electricity-generating cell, usually consisting of a modified muscle cell

Electroplaque stack or column of ELECTROCYTES; also referred to as electroplates

Endangered species SPECIES whose POPULATION has fallen to such a low level that it is at risk of EXTINCTION

Endemic term used to describe a SPECIES that is found in just one country or area

Endostyle longitudinal mucus-secreting groove found in the pharynx of sea squirts and relatives, lancelets, and lamprey LARVAE

Endothermic term used to describe animals that can generate internal body heat, e.g., mammals, birds, and certain fish like large tunas or some species of sharks

Erectile capable of being raised

Esca modified fleshy tissue on the tip of the first RAY of the DORSAL FIN (ILICIUM) in marine anglerfish; the esca resembles a small piece of "bait" that, when waved in the water, attracts PREY toward the anglerfish

Estivation dormancy or torpor during summer periods of heat and drought

Evolution development of living things by gradual changes in their characteristics as a result of MUTATION

Exotic term used to describe a SPECIES that is found in locations outside its natural distribution range, usually as a result of intentional or accidental introduction

Extant term used to describe SPECIES that are still in existence

Extinct term used to describe SPECIES that are no longer in existence

Extinction complete dying out of a SPECIES

Falcate sickle-shaped, as in the PECTORAL FINS of thresher sharks

Family group of closely related SPECIES (e.g., piranhas) or a pair of fish and their offspring

Fin winglike or paddlelike organ attached to certain parts of the body of a fish or other aquatic animals and used for steering, locomotion, and balance

Fontanel space or gap between some bones of the skull

Food chain sequence in which one organism becomes food for another, which in turn is eaten by another

Fry young fish

Fusiform body shape that tapers at both ends, i.e., spindle shaped

Ganoid scale SCALE found in most extinct ray-finned fish (Actinopterygii) consisting of a thick enamel-like layer underlaid by a dentine layer and a basal bony layer

Genus (*pl.* **genera**) group of closely related SPECIES

Gill organ by which a fish absorbs dissolved oxygen from the water and gets rid of carbon dioxide

Gill raker bristlelike extensions on the gill arches of filter-feeding fish; used for trapping suspended food particles in the water as it passes from the mouth via the GILLS and, subsequently, to the exterior through the GILL SLITS

Gill slit slit between the GILLS that allows water through

Gonopodium modified ANAL FIN of male LIVEBEARERS used to inseminate females

Habitat place where an animal or plant lives

Harem breeding "unit" consisting of a single male and several females, as in boxfish

Hemoglobin pigment that gives blood its red color; hemoglobin is used to carry oxygen around the body

Herbivore animal whose diet consists exclusively of plants

Hermaphrodite organism having both male and female reproductive organs

Heterocercal term used to describe a tail (CAUDAL FIN) in which the upper lobe contains the tip of the vertebral column (backbone); in such fins the upper lobe is usually considerably larger than the lower lobe

Holotype specimen on which the scientific description of a SPECIES is based; also referred to as the TYPE SPECIMEN

Hybrid offspring of a mating between two different SPECIES

Hydrostatic organ organ used in controlling flotation or buoyancy

Hypertrophy excessive growth as a result of an increase in cell size

Hypocercal term used to describe a tail (CAUDAL FIN) in which the lower lobe contains the end tip of the NOTOCHORD; in such fins the ventral (lower) lobe is usually larger than the dorsal (upper) one

Ichthyologist scientist specializing in the study of fish

Ilicium first modified ray of the DORSAL FIN in marine anglerfish, usually located on top of the head and bearing a fleshy tip (ESCA) used to lure unsuspecting victims toward the waiting anglerfish

Inferior mouth mouth located below the snout

Interoperculum bone joined anteriorly to the preoperculum and posteriorly to the interoperculum ligament, which, in turn, is connected to the OPERCULUM (gill cover)

Introduced describes a species that has been brought from places where it occurs naturally to places where it has not previously occurred

Invertebrate general term used to describe an animal that lacks a backbone

IUCN International Union for the Conservation of Nature, responsible for assigning animals and plants to internationally agreed categories of rarity (see table beow)

Juvenile young animal that has not reached breeding age

Krill tiny, shrimplike crustacean

Labyrinth organ respiratory organ found in gouramis and their relatives; formed from modified GILLS and housed in a chamber in the top of the gill cavity

Larva first stage of some fish SPECIES; newly hatched INVERTEBRATE

Lateral relating to the sides

Lateral line organ series of small fluid-filled pits linked to tubes that, in turn, are linked to a common canal; the lateral line detects movements (vibrations) in the water

Leptocephalus elongate, highly compressed, ribbonlike LARVAL stage of some fish such as eels

Livebearer SPECIES in which males introduce sperm into the body of the female, resulting in internal fertilization; developing embryos are generally retained by the female until birth

Macula neglecta part of the inner ear of sharks and related fish; important in sound perception

Melanoblast cell in which melanin (dark pigment) is formed

Mermaid's purse term used to describe the hard, leathery egg cases of sharks, skates, and rays

Metamorphosis changes undergone by an animal as it develops from the embryonic to the ADULT stage

Microphthalmic having tiny eyes

Migration movement of animals from one part of the world to another at different times of year to reach food or find a place to breed

Milt fluid containing male sperm

Monotype sole member of a GENUS

Monotypic GENUS or FAMILY that contains a single SPECIES

Mouthbrooder SPECIES in which the eggs are incubated in the mouth of one or other of the parents, according to species; FRY may also be protected this way

Mutation change in the genetic material (DNA) that, in turn, results in a change in a particular characteristic of an individual cell or organism

Nape the back of the neck

Naris (*pl.* **nares**) alternative word for nostril(s)

Nasopharyngeal duct nasal opening (nostril) in hagfish; also called the nasohypophysial opening

Natural selection process whereby individuals with the most appropriate ADAPTATIONS survive to produce offspring

Nematocyst stinging cell of sea anemones, jellyfish, and their relatives

Neoteny retention of larval characteristics into the sexually mature adult stage

Neural spine bone extension on the upper (dorsal) surface of individual vertebrae (back bones)

Niche part of a HABITAT occupied by a SPECIES, defined in terms of all aspects of its lifestyle (e.g., food, competitors, PREDATORS, and other resource requirements)

Nocturnal active at night

Notochord "rod" of cells along the back during the early stages of embryonic development in chordates; the notochord is replaced by the spinal column in all but the most primitive chordates

Nucleus dark, dense structure found in living cells of higher animals and plants, e.g., not in bacteria; the nucleus contains the CHROMOSOMES, which, in turn, contain genetic information in the form of DNA

Nuptial tubercle small, whitish, pimplelike growth developed by males during the breeding season, usually on the snout, head, cheeks and PECTORAL FINS; nuptial tubercles are known in at least 25 families of fish

Olfactory relating to the sense of smell

Olfactory bulb outgrowth from part of the lower anterior margin of the brain; responsible for detecting smells; also known as the OLFACTORY LOBE

Olfactory lobe see OLFACTORY BULB

Olfactory sac highly folded "chamber" in front of the OLFACTORY BULB; sensitive to smells

Omnivore animal whose diet includes both animals and plants

Operculum bone forming the gill cover in fish

Orbital relating to the eyes

Order level of taxonomic ranking

Organ of Hunter organ consisting of ELECTROCYTES that generate powerful electric pulses

Organ of Sachs organ consisting of ELECTROCYTES that are capable of generating weak electric pulses

Osmoregulation control of water balance in the body

Osmosis passage of molecules from a less concentrated to a more concentrated solution through a semipermeable membrane

Otolith grain of calcium carbonate in the semicircular canals of the ear; vital for balance

Oviparity egg laying; eggs and sperm are usually released into the environment where external fertilization takes place; in sharks the term is retained, although fertilization is internal

Ovipositor breeding tube extended by a female to place her eggs in a precise location

Palate roof of the mouth

Papilla (*pl.* **papillae**) small, usually cone-shaped projection

Parallel evolution development of similarities in separate but related evolutionary lineages through the operation of similar selective factors

Parasite organism that derives its food, for part or the whole of its life, from another living organism (belonging to a different SPECIES); parasites usually harm the organism on which they feed (the host)

Parasphenoid long, ridgelike bone with two side "arms"; located on the underside of the skull, this bone forms the "crucifix" in the crucifix fish (*Arius* spp.)

Pectoral fin one of the paired FINS connected to the pectoral girdle

Pelvic fin one of the paired FINS connected to the pelvic girdle

Pharyngeal slit alternative term for GILL SLIT

Pharyngeal teeth teeth located in the throat area and used primarily for grinding or crushing food

Pheromone substance released in tiny quantities by an animal and detected by another of the same SPECIES

Photophore luminous organ possessed by many deepwater bony and cartilaginous fish

Phylum (*pl.* **phyla**) group of animals whose basic or general plan is

IUCN CATEGORIES

EX **Extinct**, when there is no reasonable doubt that the last individual of a species has died.

EW **Extinct in the Wild**, when a species is known only to survive in captivity or as a naturalized population well outside the past range.

CR **Critically Endangered**, when a species is facing an extremely high risk of extinction in the wild in the immediate future.

EN **Endangered**, when a species faces a very high risk of extinction in the wild in the near future.

VU **Vulnerable**, when a species faces a high risk of extinction in the wild in the medium-term future.

LR **Lower Risk**, when a species has been evaluated and does not satisfy the criteria for CR, EN, or VU.

DD **Data Deficient**, when there is not enough information about a species to assess the risk of extinction.

NE **Not Evaluated**, species that have not been assessed by the IUCN criteria.

similar, and which share an evolutionary relationship, e.g., the Chordata

Phytoplankton see PLANKTON

Piscivore animal whose diet consists exclusively of fish

Placenta spongy, blood-rich tissue found in mammals and some fish, such as livebearing sharks, by which oxygen and nutrients are supplied to—and waste products are removed from—embryos during development

Placoid scale small toothlike SCALE, often referred to as a DENTICLE, found in sharks; it consists of a bonelike basal part embedded in the skin and a backward-directed free, pointed border or spine covered in an enamel-like substance; placoid scales do not increase in size as the shark grows: instead, they are replaced throughout life

Plankton term used to describe the generally minute animals (zooplankton) and plants (phytoplankton) that drift in marine and fresh water

Plica fold or wrinkle, e.g., on the skin or a membrane

Poikilothermic term used to describe animals whose body temperature matches that of the environment, e.g., most fish, amphibians, and reptiles; such animals are frequently—but inaccurately—referred to as cold-blooded

Polyp individual animal making up a colony, as in corals; polyps have a tubular body, usually topped by a tentacle-ringed mouth, giving the animal the appearance of a miniature sea anemone

Polyploidy process by which cells possess three or more full sets of chromosomes

Population distinct group of animals of the same SPECIES or all the animals of that species

Postanal tail tail whose base originates behind the anus

Predator animal that hunts and kills other animals for food

Preoperculum anterior bone of the gill cover

Prey animal hunted for food

Proboscis elongated trunklike snout or projection

Protandrous hermaphrodite hermaphrodite that goes through a male phase before becoming a female

Protogynous hermaphrodite hermaphrodite that goes through a female phase before becoming a male

Protractile describes any structure that can be lengthened by, e.g., being pushed out, as spiny-finned fish are able to do with their mouths

Race see SUBSPECIES

Radial muscle muscle associated with the FIN RAYS of the head (known as radials)

Range geographical area over which an organism is distributed

Ray small spine that acts as a

support for the FIN membrane

Recruitment addition of new individuals to a population, usually by reproduction or by inward migration from another population

Refractive index degree by which light rays are "bent" as they pass from one medium to another, e.g., from air to water

Rete mirabile dense network of blood vessels found in certain animals; heat exchange can occur between blood across this network allowing, e.g,. some sharks to retain body heat and maintain their internal temperature at a higher level than that of the surrounding water

Retina inner, light-sensitive layer of the eye on which images are formed

Reverse countershading type of color distribution seen in fish SPECIES that habitually swim upside down, e.g., some members of the Mochokidae; in these fish the belly is darker than the back, i.e., it shows the opposite color distribution found in normally COUNTERSHADED fish

Rod rod-shaped light-sensitive cell in the retina of the eye; rods are particularly sensitive to discerning shapes, especially in dim light (see CONE)

Rostral associated with a snout or ROSTRUM

Rostrum snout

Rugosity term used to describe rough or wrinkled tissue

Scale one of the usually tough, flattish plates that form part of the external covering of most fish species

Scatophagous term used to describe an animal that feeds on waste materials like sewage or feces; best-known fish exhibiting this trait are the scats

Scute platelike, modified scales found in some fish, including catfish

Semicircular canal fluid-filled canal in the inner ear; semicircular canals are set at right angles to each other, contain OTOLITHS, and are essential in maintaining body balance

Shell gland gland possessed by female sharks, skates, and rays; responsible for secreting the outer egg casing known as a MERMAID'S PURSE

Siphon funnel-shaped structure through which water can be taken in (inhalant) or discharged (exhalant)

Spawn eggs of a fish; the act of producing eggs

Species a POPULATION or series of populations that interbreed freely but not normally with those of other species

Specific gravity (SG) "weight," or density, of a liquid compared with pure water at 39.2° F (4° C); pure water has an SG value of 1.000, while the SG of seawater is around 1.020

Spiracle porelike opening associated with the GILLS

Spiral valve spiral infolding of the intestinal wall in primitive fish like sharks and rays

Standard length (SL) length of a fish measured from the tip of the snout to the CAUDAL PEDUNCLE

Stridulation vibration or rubbing together of two surfaces to produce a sound; in fish it usually refers to rubbing together of bones or fin spines, e.g., in some filefish and triggerfish

Stripping removal of eggs and sperm from ripe fish by the application of gentle pressure along the abdomen

Suborbital located under the orbit, or eye socket

Subphylum grouping of organisms sharing a number of characteristics in addition to those shared by members of a PHYLUM; examples of a subphylum are the sea squirts and relatives (Urochordata) and the backboned animals (VERTEBRATA), which together form the phylum CHORDATA

Subspecies subdivision of a SPECIES that is distinguishable from the rest of that species; often called a RACE

Substrate bottom of an aquatic HABITAT

Subterminal located underneath the end or tip, e.g., a subterminal mouth is one located underneath the tip of the snout

Suprabranchial chamber cavity or space above the gill chamber; the suprabranchial chamber houses the suprabranchial organ, i.e., modified gill tissues used by air-breathing fish, such as walking catfish

Supraorbital located above the orbit, or eye socket

Suture line along which two or more bones are immovably joined, as in the skull

Swim bladder gas-filled sac found in the body cavity of most bony fish; the amount of gas in the swim bladder can be regulated, allowing the fish to rise or sink in the water

Symbiosis relationship between two unrelated organisms from which both parties benefit, e.g., the light-producing bacteria that flashlight fish have in special cheek pouches (light organs); organisms that live in this manner are referred to as symbionts

Symphysis junction between the left and right sides of the jaw, i.e., where both bones meet and fuse at the front

Tapetum lucidum layer of light-reflecting tissue located under the retina; it amplifies the amount of light entering the eye and assists vision under poor light conditions

Taxonomy studying, naming, and grouping of living organisms; also termed classification

Tendril entwining, fiberlike extension on some shark and ray egg cases that allows the eggs to attach themselves to underwater objects like seaweeds

Terminal located at the end or tip, e.g., a terminal mouth is one located at the tip of the snout

Territory area that an animal or

animals consider their own and defend against others

Thermocline zone between warm surface water and colder deeper layers

Tholichthys term used to describe the young of certain fish, notably the scats, for a period after hatching; these larvae have large heads in relation to the body and protective bony plates and spines

Thoracic describes the area in or around the chest (thorax)

Thunniform swimming swimming technique in which the tail beats rapidly from side to side, but the body remains rigid; this type of swimming is found in tunas

Tonic immobility trancelike state or hypnosis exhibited by many animals, including some sharks and their relatives

Total length (TL) length of a fish measured from the tip of the snout to the tip of the CAUDAL FIN

T-position position adopted by at least some *Corydoras* species during mating, in which the female aligns herself at right angles to her mate's body, with her mouth close to his genital aperture

Truncated term often used to describe a CAUDAL FIN that has a straight, or more-or-less straight, edge

Tubercle small rounded swelling, nodule, or protuberance, as found, e.g., on the body of banjo catfish

Type specimen see HOLOTYPE

Uterine milk nutritious secretions produced in the womb (uterus) of female sharks during pregnancy; developing embryos feed on these secretions

Uterus womb

Variety occasional variation in a species not sufficiently persistent or geographically separate to form a SUBSPECIES

Ventral relating to the underside

Vertebra any of the bones of the spinal column

Vertebrata SUBPHYLUM of the PHYLUM Chordata characterized, especially, by a brain enclosed in a skull (cranium) and having a backbone (vertebral column) enclosing the spinal cord

Viviparity alternative term for LIVEBEARING

Weberian apparatus series of four small bones connecting the swim bladder to the ear in some fish (superorder Ostariophysi), including the catfish

World Conservation Union see IUCN

Yolk sac source of nourishment for some FRY prior to and immediately after hatching

Zooplankton see PLANKTON

Further Reading

General
Allen, G. R., *Freshwater Fishes of Australia*, T. F. H. Publications, Inc., Neptune City, NJ, 1989

Bond, C. E., *Biology of Fishes*, Saunders College Publishing, Philadelphia, PA, 1979

Campbell, A., and Dawes, J. (eds.), *The New Encyclopedia of Aquatic Life* Facts on File, New York, NY, 2004

Gilbert, C. R., and Williams, J. D., *National Audubon Society Field Guide to Fishes*, Alfred A. Knopf, New York, NY, 2002

Hayward, P., Nelson-Smith, T., and Sheilds, C., *Collins Pocket Guide to Sea Shore of Britain and Europe,* HarperCollins, London, U.K., 1996

Helfman, G. S., Collette, B. B., and Facey, D. E., *The Diversity of Fishes*, Blackwell Scientific Publications, Cambridge, MA, 1997

Meinkoth, N. A., *National Audubon Society Field Guide to North American Seashore Creatures*, Alfred A. Knopf, New York, NY, 1998

Moyle, P. B., and Cech, J. J. Jr., *Fishes: An Introduction to Ichthyology* (4th edn.), Prentice-Hall, Inc., Upper Saddle River, NJ, 2000

Nelson, J. S., *Fishes of the World* (3rd edn.), John Wiley and Sons, Inc., New York, NY, 1994

Page, L. M., and Burr, B. M. *A Field Guide to Freshwater Fishes (North America, North of Mexico)* (Peterson Field Guide Series), Houghton Mifflin Co., Boston, MA, 1991

Paxton, J. R., and Eschmeyer, W. N., *Encyclopedia of Fishes* (2nd edn.), Academic Press, San Diego, CA, 1998

Spotte, S., *Captive Seawater Fishes*, John Wiley & Sons, Inc., New York, NY, 1992

Specific to this volume
Dawes, J., *Complete Encyclopedia of the Freshwater Aquarium,* Firefly Books Ltd, Richmond Hill, Canada, 2001

Lever, C., *Naturalized Fishes of the World,* Academic Press, San Diego, CA/London, U.K., 1996

Michaels, V. K., *Carp Farming*, Fishing News Books, Farnham, U.K., 1988

Ono, R. D., Williams, J. D., and Wagner, A., *Vanishing Fishes of North America*, Stone Wall Press, Inc., Washington, D.C.,1983

Pecl, K., Hisek, K., and Maly, J., *Fishes of Lakes and Rivers* (Magna Colour Guide), Magna Books, Leicester, U.K., 1995

Smartt, J., *Goldfish Varieties and Genetics: Handbook for Breeders*, Fishing News Books, Oxford, U.K., 2001

Wheeler, A., *The Pocket Guide to Freshwater Fishes of Britain and Europe*, Dragon's World, Limpsfield, U.K., 1992

Winfield, I. J., and Nelson, J. S. (eds.), *Cyprinid Fishes: Systematics, Biology and Exploitation* (Fish & Fisheries Series 3), Chapman & Hall, London, U.K., 1991

Useful Websites

http://www.fishbase.org/home.htm
An amazing website full of information even on obscure fish, with copious references to other sources

http://www.si.edu/resource/faq/nmnh/fish.htm
A useful list of alternative reference for all kinds of fish

http://www.ucmp.berkeley.edu/vertebrates/basalfish/chondrintro.html
Covers both fossil and living species, with good links

Picture Credits

Abbreviations A Ardea, London; BCL Bruce Coleman Limited; FLPA Frank Lane Picture Agency; NHPA Natural History Photographic Agency; NPL Naturepl.com; P Photomax; P.com/OSF Photolibrary.com/Oxford Scientific Films; SPL Science Photo Library
t = top; b = bottom; c = center; l = left; r = right

Jacket tl Gerard Lacz/FLPA; tr David Fleetham/P.com/OSF; bl Jeff Rotman/NPL; br Paul Kay/P.com/OSF

8–9 Foto Natura Stock/FLPA; 10–11, 12-13 Max Gibbs/P; 14–15 Max Gibbs/P.com/OSF; 17, 18–19 Max Gibbs/P; 21 Keith Martin-Smith; 22–23, 24–25, 26, 27, 28, 29 Max Gibbs/P; 30–31 Pat Morris/A; 33 Brian Bevan/A; 34 Tim Martin/NPL; Colin Milkins/P.com/OSF; 36 Foto Natura Stock/FLPA; 38–39, 40–41, 40t, 43,44, 45t, 45, 46, 47, 48, 49, 51, 53, 55t, 55b, 56–57 Max Gibbs/P; 59 Lutra/NHPA; 60–61, 61t, 62t, 62–63, 64–65 Max Gibbs/P; 66–67 Peter Gathercole/P.com/OSF; 67 Max Gibbs/P; 69, 70t, 70–71 Nature's Images Inc; 73 Colin Milkins/P.com/OSF; 74, 75, 76–77 Max Gibbs/P; 78–79 Breck P. Kent/P.com/OSF; 81 Naturbild/NPL; 82–83 Max Gibbs/P; 85 Martin H Smith/NPL; 86 Colin Milkins/P.com/OSF; 87 Max Gibbs/P; 88–89 Gerard Lacz/FLPA; 91 Peter Gathercole/P.com/OSF; 92–93, 95 Max Gibbs/P; 96–97, 98–99 Nature's Images Inc; 100–101, 103, 104–105, 105t, 107, 108–109 Max Gibbs/P; 111 Pat Morris/A

Artists Denys Ovenden, Mick Loates, Colin Newman

Set Index

A **bold** number shows the volume and is followed by the relevant page numbers (eg., **37:** 8, 70).

Common names in **bold** mean that the fish (e.g., **shark, great white**) or group or family of fish (e.g., **sheatfish**) has an illustrated main entry in the set. Underlined page numbers (e.g., **37:** 36–37) refer to the main entry for that fish or group.

Italic page numbers (e.g., **37:** 49) point to illustrations of fish in parts of the set other than the main entry.

Page numbers in parentheses—e.g., **34:** (87)—locate information in At-a-glance boxes.

Fish or families or groups of fish with main entries in the set are indexed under their common names, alternative common names, and scientific names.